The Funniest People in Neighborhoods: 250 Anecdotes

David Bruce

Published by David Bruce, 2022.

While every precaution has been taken in the preparation of this book, the publisher assumes no responsibility for errors or omissions, or for damages resulting from the use of the information contained herein.

THE FUNNIEST PEOPLE IN NEIGHBORHOODS: 250 ANECDOTES

First edition. October 4, 2022.

ISBN: 979-8215918661

Written by David Bruce.

Table of Contents

Dedication

Dedicated to My Sister Brenda

Brenda wrote, "During COVID and when visitors were restricted from visiting their loved one in the assisted-living facility I worked at, a patient mentioned to me how much she liked spaghetti during a late-night conversation we had. She was a night owl like me. Her name was Dee. I called her "Gerdy." Then she would say, "Dirty Gerdy," and we'd laugh. On my way to work I bought two spaghetti meals from Olive Garden. I left for work early that night. I went to work, set up outlet dinners in the dining room, went to her room and wheeled her down to the dining room where we had dinner together. At that time, the residents weren't leaving their room and had their meals alone in their room. It was nighttime and everyone was already in bed, so I didn't see a problem. She was so grateful and had enough food for three more meals. It was such a simple gesture, but during that time it meant so much to her and for me."

Brenda once bought a newspaper at a gas station on Thanksgiving and tipped the female employee $5, and the employee cried.

Brenda wrote, "I do remember that. I also remember when George tipped a TeeJays waitress $100, and she cried. Our family does a lot of good deeds all the time: I unload people's grocery carts when the people are in those electric scooters. If they are alone with a few groceries, I'll leave cash for the cashier to pay for the groceries. I've had a lot of good deeds done to me when I didn't have a lot of money. It feels good to pay it forward."

She added, "I just have one more thing to add and then I'm done. I've had a lot of people in my life do good deeds for me when I was at a low point on my life. I was at a low point for a very long time. David, you know what you've done for me, and I can never thank you enough. Martha paid for antibiotics for me when I had strep throat and didn't have money. Rosa bought me groceries. Carla has done so much, and she had us over for Easter just after Chad died. When I say US, I mean all of my kids. She was so sick and ended up at the Emergency Room that same night. Frank gave me a car. And George buys my gas for me whenever he's in Florida. And Mom and Dad were good people. I had a lot of good influences in my life that made me be a good person. At least I hope I'm a good person. I try to be someone Mom and Dad would be proud of."

In a booklet she wrote about Hospice, Brenda wrote, "I used to send flowers to the funeral home, but years ago during the loss of my stepson, someone showed up to our door with a laundry basket of essential items: paper plates, plastic cups, trash bags, beverages, dish liquid, washing powder, napkins, and paper towels. Items I never knew we even needed until we needed them. Paper products are essential during this time. I have adopted this idea and now use it whenever we suffer the loss of a friend. I fill a laundry basket full of these essential items. We may also give restaurant gift cards to cover a dinner for an evening."

Brenda also wrote, "I was a Hospice nurse for a patient in a facility, and I asked the nurse on duty to medicate my patient. She said she didn't need it as she was sleeping, and the medications were PRN (as needed). I explained that she needed the medications. She said she can't justify giving her medications. I said it's called symptoms management. She said the patient will need to ask for the medication herself. I tried to educate the nurse, but she was offended and left the room. It's important to be polite but firm. I make no apologies when I am advocating for someone who needs me. I had to call the Hospice doctor, who in turn called the facility nurse who quickly and efficiently medicated the patient as requested. Let's face it, we're not here to make friends. If it takes rudeness to do what's right, I'll be rude."

***

The doing of good deeds is important. As a free person, you can choose to live your life as a good person or as a bad person. To be a good person, do good deeds. To be a bad person, do bad deeds. If you do good deeds, you will become good. If you do bad deeds, you will become bad. To become the person you want to be, act as if you already are that kind of person. Each of us chooses what kind of person we will become. To become a good person, do the things a good person does. To become a bad person, do the things a bad person does. The opportunity to take action to become the kind of person you want to be is yours.

Cover Photograph for *The Funniest People in Neighborhoods: 250 Anecdotes*

https://pixabay.com/photos/woman-young-girlie-playing-cello-8009216/

NOTE: The young woman is cool rather than funny, but I love this photo and want to use it.

All anecdotes have been retold in my own words
to avoid plagiarism.

Anecdotes are usually short humorous stories. Sometimes they are thought-provoking or informative, not amusing.

Chapter 1: From Alcohol to Children

Alcohol

• During a long-distance telephone call, choreographer Agnes de Mille told her soldier husband, Walter Prude, that she was pregnant: "We're having a baby!" He managed to say, "Good God, are you sure!" before they were disconnected — telephone service during World War II was not as good as it is today. Twenty-five minutes later, they were reconnected, and Agnes asked, "Are you all right? Have you something to drink?" Walter replied, "A bottle of Scotch. I'm well along in it."[1]

• Before they were married, Fred and Joanne Rogers (TV's Mister Rogers and his significant other) went to many dances and parties, and they once won a bottle of champagne for their costumes when they went as Raggedy Ann and Andy. Because they were teetotalers, they did not drink it, but instead went around pouring it at various tables for their friends.[2]

Animals

• A few months after African-American contralto Marian Anderson had been prevented from singing at Constitution Hall in Washington, D.C., because of her race, Pierre Monteux and the San Francisco Symphony Orchestra were scheduled to perform there. Doris, Pierre's wife, arrived, along with Fifi, their pet dog. Unfortunately, three stern-looking men stopped Doris, telling her that under no circumstances could she enter Constitution Hall with "that dog." A friend of Doris, Hilda Davis, told the stern-looking men, "Without a doubt we cannot enter because the dog, as you call her, is BLACK." As Ms. Davis and the stern-looking men argued, Doris and Fifi made their way into Constitution Hall, where they enjoyed the concert.[3]

• Marion Dane Bauer, author of the 1987 Newbery Honor Book titled *On My Honor*, has trained herself to be observant of behavior, including animal behavior. For example, she watched Popcorn, her pet dog, looking at snow. Popcorn first looked outside the kitchen window and watched snow falling. Then Popcorn looked down the hallway and through the dining-room glass doors and watched snow falling. Then Popcorn looked up at the ceiling. Clearly, Popcorn was wondering why white stuff was falling in front of the house and in back of the house but not in the house.[4]

• When she was in the first grade, children's book author Lois Lowry found what she thought was a very cold mouse. (Actually, it was a dead rat, but she didn't understand such things yet.) Hoping to warm up the "mouse" and keep it as a pet, she took it home, put it in the oven, and turned the oven on to a low temperature. Then she started playing and forgot about her new pet. Her mother noticed that something was being baked in the oven, and she checked it out — then, Lois says, her mother started screaming at her for no reason.[5]

• Even a dog can be a critic. Famed architect Frank Lloyd Wright designed a number of mansions, but he also designed a number of modest houses. After schoolteacher Robert Berger built his own house using Mr. Wright's design, his 12-year-old son wrote Mr. Wright asking him to design a matching doghouse. Mr. Wright did exactly that, and Mr. Berger and his son built the doghouse. However, Eddie, their Labrador retriever, apparently did not like the doghouse and so never went into it.[6]

• In 1924, Pep, a black Labrador retriever, killed a cat that belonged to the governor of Pennsylvania. The governor was not pleased. Because he was a judge, he decided to hold a trial for Pep. He found Pep guilty, and Pep was sent to prison for life. However, Pep was happy in prison. He was allowed to run free as he pleased, and he accompanied the prisoners on their work details. Pep liked the prisoners, and the prisoners liked Pep. When Pep finally died, prisoners wept.[7]

• In his book *Faith, Hope, and Hilarity*, Dick Van Dyke tells a story about a boy who prayed to God to bring him a puppy. Unfortunately, his mother was allergic to dogs and so she got him a kitten instead. The boy told his mother, "I thought you said that God is perfect and never makes mistakes." "That's true," his mother said. "Well, you're wrong," her son said. "I prayed real hard for a puppy and *anyone* can see that this is a kitten."[8]

• At a Westminster Dog Show in Madison Square Garden, a woman was selling an expensive coat made for dogs. Saying "We want her dog to look as smart as madame," the saleslady held up a pink cocktail coat made out of embroidered silk with a lining of mohair. Sportswriter Robert Lipsyte asked her, "When would a dog wear that?" The saleslady replied, "After five o'clock."[9]

• When opera singer Joan Hammond returned to Australia for a visit, two of her nieces asked for her autograph — in fact, they each gave her a piece of paper and asked that she sign each piece of paper ten times. When she had finished, they said, "Goody! Now we can swap these for twenty tadpoles!"[10]

Art

• Shortly after Vincent van Gogh died, Theo, his brother, followed him in death. Nearly everyone thought that Vincent had been a failure as an artist, and Theo's widow, Jo, was urged by her brother to throw away Vincent's paintings and other works of art. She declined to do that. Instead, she preserved Vincent's works of art and the letters that he and Theo had written to each other over the years. She organized exhibitions, wrote a biography of Vincent, and arranged for the publication of the letters. Without her efforts, many soon-to-be-recognized-as-masterpieces works of art would have perished.[11]

• In 1962, sculptor Louise Nevelson traveled to Italy to represent the United States in the Biennale Internazionale d'Arte in Venice. Unfortunately, her trousseau turned up missing, and the airline officials had little interest in locating it for her. Of course, she did not want to wear her traveling clothes at such an important competition. Therefore, she lied to the airline official, "I'm getting married tomorrow, and I've got to have my trousseau. My white wedding dress is in it!" The airline official started making telephone calls and soon the trousseau was located for the 62-year-old "bride."[12]

• Vincent van Gogh once gave a painting to a friend named Anton Kerssemakers, who pointed out that he hadn't signed the painting. Mr. van Gogh replied, "Actually, it isn't necessary — they will surely recognize my work later on and write about me when I am dead and gone."[13]

• Pop artist Andy Warhol was a cat person. He and his mother kept a couple of dozen cats in the apartment they shared together. All of the cats were named Sam.[14]

Babies

• When children's book author Tomie DePaola was in kindergarten, his parents brought home a baby sister for him. At the baby's baptism, little Tomie saw the priest pour water on his baby sister's head, and so he wanted water poured on his head. Hearing him, the priest promised, "Little boy, if you're quiet you can have anything you want after the ceremony." Knowing little Tomie, his dad said, "Big mistake, Father." Tomie was quiet, and when the priest asked what he wanted after the ceremony, Tomie said, "Baby Jesus," by which he meant the baby Jesus in the church's nativity scene. Of course, Tomie couldn't have that particular baby Jesus, but his parents bought him another one at Woolworth's.[15]

• When a family had a baby, their young son insisted on having a private time with the new baby. Of course, the parents were afraid that their young son was jealous of the new baby and might try to hurt it, so they unobtrusively hid and watched their young son as he was "alone" with the new baby. However, the boy did not try to hurt the baby. All he did was request, "Tell me what it was like. I'm beginning to forget."[16]

• Jimmy Piersall was a Red Sox outfielder who had 10 children and was intimately familiar with changing cloth diapers, so he had the perfect qualifications to teach Yankee catcher Yogi Berra how to diaper a child: "Yog, you take a diaper and put it in the shape of a baseball diamond. Take the baby's bottom and put it on the pitcher's mound. Take first base and pin it to third. Take home and slide it to second."[17]

Birth

• Marty Links was a woman who created a comic strip titled *Bobby Sox* about a teenager. She was a member of the National Cartoonists Society, and after giving birth to her first child, she mailed the members of the NCS an announcement, so she was somewhat annoyed when they kept sending her mail addressed to Mr. Links. (She even considered sending them her measurements in an attempt to get them to get her sex right.)[18]

• In 1969, New York Met Ron Swoboda became a proud father. The birth occurred back home in New York at 1 a.m. at the same time that Mr. Swoboda was playing an away game in Los Angeles at 10 p.m. due to the three-hour time difference on the coasts. On the scoreboard flashed this message: "Congratulations, Ron Swoboda. Your new son was born tomorrow morning."[19]

Birthdays

• William C. McVeigh and his wife, Ruth, live in Fountain Hills, Arizona, where they had 14 children. Three of their children, Robert, Charles, and James, were born on December 4, but in different years. As the boys were growing up, each year on their birthday the family would bring a birthday cake, sing "Happy Birthday" to Bobby, then take four candles off the cake and sing "Happy Birthday" to Charlie, and finally take three more candles off the cake and sing "Happy Birthday" to Jimmy.[20]

• When Yoshiko Uchida, author of *Journey to Topaz*, was a little girl, her grandmother celebrated her 88th birthday. Little Yoshiko worried about how her grandmother would blow out all those candles on her birthday cake, but when the time came, her grandmother simply took a fan and with one sweep of her arm blew out all the candles. (Her grandmother was always prepared. In her closet was a very nice black dress. Pinned on it was this note: "This one is for my trip to Heaven.")[21]

Books

• When children's mystery writer Joan Lowery Nixon was a little girl, she found a stack of magazines — with such titles as *True Confessions*, *True Love*, and *Modern Romances* — in a box under her grandmother's bed. Being an avid reader, she avidly began to read. That night, at supper, she asked her parents the meanings of a few words she had read in the magazines but had not understood. Surprised, her parents asked her where she had come across such words, and the story of the box of magazines came out. Her grandfather, a self-educated lover of the classics, blamed himself for not educating the mind of his wife, and announced that he would read to her that night a story from *The Arabian Nights: Tales from a Thousand and One Nights*. The reading did not go well. He started to read "The Porter and the Three Ladies of Baghdad," but when he read out loud that one of the three ladies had breasts "like two pomegranates of even size," his wife was outraged. She stormed, "Twin pomegranates! Oh, how rude! There is nothing that vulgar in my magazines!" And so Ms. Nixon's grandmother's education in the classics came to an end.[22]

• Jean Little, the author of *Little by Little*, once read *The Secret Garden* to some children she was babysitting. The girls seemed very interested in the book, so she read a couple of extra chapters, but the boy looked bored. However, after Ms. Little had finished reading, the boy wanted to use the telephone. Given permission, he called his mother and said in an excited tone, "Mum, they got into the garden!" Ms. Little learned from this experience: "Never again did I make the mistake of thinking that a child who appeared inattentive was getting nothing out of a book."[23]

Children

• Determined to found a new community, a king selected a site and then consulted his astrologers. The astrologers read the stars and planets, concluding that the site was good — if a child would be entombed alive within the walls of the community. Therefore, a mother was forced to "volunteer" her child to be entombed alive. However, the mother's child was very intelligent, and he told the king, "Let me ask your astrologers three questions. If the astrologers answer the questions correctly, then we will know that they can truly read the stars and planets, and I will willingly be entombed alive. However, if they answer wrongly, then we will know that they wrongly read the stars and planets, and no one should be entombed alive." The king agreed to the child's request, and the child asked the astrologers these questions: "What is the lightest thing in the world? What is the sweetest thing in the world? And what is the heaviest thing in the world?" The astrologers consulted among themselves for three days, then told their answers to the three questions: "The lightest thing in the world is a feather, the sweetest thing in the world is honey, and the heaviest thing in the world is stone." The child laughed and said, "The lightest thing in the world is an only child in its mother's arms — the child is never heavy. The sweetest thing in the world is the mother's milk to the baby. And the heaviest thing in the world is for a mother to be forced to 'volunteer' her child to be entombed alive." The astrologers recognized that the child's answers were correct, so they told the king that they had misread the stars and planets, and no one was entombed alive.[24]

• When he was a child, Daniel Keyes, author of *Flowers for Algernon*, played at his mother's beauty shop — their apartment was on the floor above. One day, a mother and her very young daughter came in, and as the mother was getting her hair done, her daughter kept crying. Young Danny tried to play with her, but nothing stopped her crying. Finally, he went upstairs, got an armload of books, and started "reading" one of the books to the young girl, who stopped crying as he said, "Once upon a time, there was a beautiful princess ...." The girl's mother was impressed and thought that young Danny could read, even though he was only three and a half years old. She even thought that he was a genius! But of course, there was a trick — his mother had read the books so many times to him that he had memorized them. Later, after Daniel was still very young but had learned how to read, his father ran a junk salvage operation. Sometimes Daniel's father took him to the junk shop, where he was fascinated by Book Mountain — a huge pile of books that were to be baled, then pulped to make cheap paper. One of Daniel's treats was to climb Book Mountain, look over the books to see which were worth saving, and take home with him six or seven books to read.[25]

• When she was very little, Sarah Hughes, the gold-winning medalist in women's figure skating at the 2002 Winter Olympic Games, was unwilling to be left behind with a sitter while her mother and older siblings went to interesting places — such as the ice skating rink. If she ever thought that she might be left behind with a sitter, she would dress herself and wait by the door. Eventually, her mother and older siblings would show up and be forced to take little Sarah with them. Being so motivated to skate helped three-year-old Sarah learn things — such as how to tie her shoes. On an early trip to the rink, her mother tied Sarah's ice skates first, and little Sarah jumped up and ran to the rink, with her mother — who was pregnant — vainly trying to catch up to her. On the next trip to the rink, her mother thought that she would tie Sarah's ice skates last; that way, Sarah would be forced to wait until her mother could keep an eye on her. It didn't work. Sarah pulled the laces tight, then concentrated. She figured out how to tie her ice skates, jumped up, and ran to the rink.[26]

• When he was three years old, children's book author Tomie dePaola attended the birthday party of Buddy, his older brother. For this party, their mother wanted to have a Tiny Tot Wedding, complete with a little groom and a littler bride. However, Buddy didn't want to be the groom, and since it was his birthday, his mother said that he didn't have to and she would ask another boy to be the groom. Unfortunately, Buddy got the other boys to say that they didn't want

to be the groom, either. That left young Tomie, who said that he was
too short to be the groom — since he was only three years old, that
was true. Nevertheless, Buddy and Tomie's mother was resourceful.
Carol Crane, the tallest girl at the party, made a wonderful groom, and
standing beside her was a shorter bride. A woman asked Buddy who the
pretty little bride was, and he replied, "That bride is my brother."[27]

• When children's book author Judy Blume was growing up, she
was very much into reading and loved the library. (She even imitated
the librarians by pasting card pockets inside the back covers of her
personal copies of books.) Her parents encouraged her to read,
although her mother told her that she had to be older to read John
O'Hara's *A Rage to Live*. When Judy was older and a junior in high
school, she was delighted to find out that she had to read a book — any
book — by John O'Hara, and she marched to the library to borrow *A
Rage to Live*. Unfortunately, the librarian told her that *A Rage to Live*
was on a restricted shelf and so Judy would have to have her mother's
written permission to borrow the book. Judy complained to her family,
and her aunt lent her a copy of the book. Judy read it, then she read
everything else she could find by Mr. O'Hara.[28]

• A man once made a will saying that his son would not be able to
inherit his wealth until he had become a fool. Such a will was puzzling,
and Rabbi Jose and Rabbi Judah decided to consult Rabbi Joshua
about it. When Rabbi Jose and Rabbi Judah arrived at the house of
Rabbi Joshua, they discovered that Rabbi Joshua was letting his young
son climb onto his back and ride on top of him as they played Horsie
together. When Rabbi Joshua learned why they had come, he said that
the will was not difficult to understand. When a man has children, he
is allowed to act foolishly — just like Rabbi Joshua had done while
playing Horsie with his son. Therefore, the will was simply saying that
the dead man's son could not inherit the dead man's property until the
son had children of his own.[29]

• As a little girl, author Beth Lisick suffered an accident in which she became a bloody mess after a butcher knife accidentally flew out of her brother's hand and struck her in the corner of her eye. Blood flowed freely, and her mother took her to the emergency room and got her stitched up, then took her home. However, Beth had a weird sense of humor, so she snuck out of her house instead of taking a bath, and caked with blood, she rang the doorbell of her best friend, Amy, and scared her best friend's mother by looking psychotic, raising a knife (which she had "borrowed" without permission) in a menacing way, and asking, "Can Amy come out to play?" By the way, when a boy teased Amy, who had buck teeth, by giving her the nickname "Buck Tooth Beaver," Beth stood up for her friend by kicking the boy in a place that earned her a special nickname: The Nutcracker.[30]

• The children of famed architect Frank Lloyd Wright were entirely normal. As teenagers, his daughters used to sit by the fireplace and hold hands with their boyfriends. Their younger brothers used to sneak up on them and throw wadded-up paper at them. Mr. Wright used a very large room as a bedroom for all of his children. The bedroom had a low partition in the middle, and the girls slept on one side of the partition, while the boys slept on the other side. When the girls had a slumber party, the boys threw pillows at them over the low partition. And when Mr. Wright built a studio onto his house so he could work at home with his employees, his children would sneak onto a balcony overlooking the studio and throw things at their father's draftsmen.[31]

• The oldest child of children's book author Lois Lowry is Alix, who attended nursery school when she was almost five years old. While picking up Alix one day, Lois carried her youngest child, a newborn named Ben. Alix's teacher was surprised to see Ben, saying, "I didn't know Alix had a baby brother. When we talked about families at Circle Time, she told us she was the only child in the family." Then she said that of course Ben was a newborn, so Alix had been a single child when she spoke about her family. Actually, Alix had not been a single child then, for two other children were between Alix and Ben. But Alix wanted to be the only child — the center of attention — and for a while in nursery school, she was.[32]

• Christian writer Dale Hanson Bourke became concerned when a four-year-old bully named Brian hit her four-year-old son, named Chase, in the playground. She had been hearing from her son that Brian had been doing bad things, so she advised, "If he ever does that to you again, just hit him right back!" Chase, however, was unwilling: "But, Mom, that might make him cry." This comment helped Ms. Bourke to calm down. A few days later she learned that young Brian's parents were involved in a messy divorce case, contributing to his bad behavior, and so she and her son prayed for Brian. Because of the seriousness of the situation, young Chase prayed first to Jesus, and then to God.[33]

• When Yoshiko Uchida, author of *Journey to Topaz*, was a little girl growing up in California, she disliked some of the visitors to her home. After hearing of a Japanese superstition that stated to get rid of unwanted visitors you should put a cloth over the bristles of a broom then lean it upside down against a wall, she decided to try it. It worked — the unwanted visitor left quickly. However, Yoshiko's mother was horrified by what she had done. For one thing, she had placed the broom where the visitor could see it. The Japanese-ancestry visitor realized that he was not wanted there (by Yoshiko, at least) and left.[34]

• In 1958, the Brooklyn Dodgers moved to Los Angeles. This was an important event, for major-league baseball had finally arrived in the western part of the continental United States. Players and their family members were interviewed by the media, and Danny, the nine-year-old son of Dodger pitcher Carl Erskine, even made an appearance on Art Linkletter's TV show *Kids Say the Darnest Things*. Mr. Linkletter asked Danny what his father did for a living, and Danny explained, "Oh, he doesn't work — he plays for the Dodgers." And when Mr. Linkletter asked what the letters "LA" stood for on the Dodgers baseball caps, Danny answered, "Lost Again."[35]

• Jerry Spinelli, author of the Newbery Award-winning young people's novel *Maniac Magee*, at first wrote novels — which were unpublished — for adults. However, one evening, he packed chicken in his lunch bag, and the next day he went to the refrigerator to get his lunch. When he opened the bag, he found chicken bones. He realized that one of his children must have eaten the chicken, he thought the situation was funny, and he began to write about it from a child's point of view. Using this scene as his initial inspiration, eventually he created his first published novel: *Space Station Second Grade*.[36]

• Elizabeth, the 11-year-old daughter of pianist Rudolf Serkin, once attended one of her father's concerts, where she ignored his playing but instead stared at the bald head of a man under the box where she was sitting. Finally, she could resist temptation no longer, so she spit directly on the bald man's head. When her father spoke to her later, telling her that she should not to do such things, she replied, "But, Father, it was the chance of a lifetime, and I could not let it pass. I'm sure *you* would have done it, also."[37]

• When he was only five years old, Dicky, the youngest son of artist Edna Hibel, had already started a "museum" in the attic of their home. There he displayed his favorite things, such as rocks, shells, photographs, and even small paintings created by his mother and given to him occasionally when he asked her for a painting to display in his museum. Once, his mother made a sale of two small paintings, and Dicky tried to stop her from selling them by grabbing her legs and yelling, "Those are the ones I wanted."[38]

• When she was a small child, Joan Moore was kept inside on a rainy day, and her mother gave her some watercolor paints and paper to keep her busy. After a while, her mother heard young Joan calling, "Come see! Come see!" When she entered the room, she discovered that Joan had gotten tired of painting paper, so she had painted herself green from the top of her head to the tips of her toes. Later, Joan used her energy and creativity to become a top-ranked American gymnast of the 1970s.[39]

• As a child, American realist painter Andrew Wyeth was called "that sinister demon child" by author Joseph Hergesheimer because young Andrew tormented him by pretending that Mr. Hergesheimer was another person: someone whom Mr. Hergesheimer detested. Young Andrew would call Mr. Hergesheimer by the other person's name, and when Mr. Hergesheimer tried to correct him, Andrew would ask, "Isn't that your name?" Mr. Hergesheimer would reply, "Not by fifty years and two cross-eyes."[40]

• When figure skater Sasha Cohen was a little girl, her misbehavior necessitated a lot of time-outs, so she was used to causing and getting into trouble. A California girl, she experienced her first earthquake while playing under the dining room table. After the earth stopped shaking, she crawled out from under the table and told her mother, "I am so sorry, Mommy. I won't ever do *that* again." Her mother explained to little Sasha that she had not caused the earthquake.[41]

• Some young children are surprised that older adults have parents, too. Librarian Jeanette C. Smith once made friends with a 10-year-old girl who often came into the Minnesota public library where she worked. One day, Ms. Smith's mother visited her, leaving as the 10-year-old girl arrived. The 10-year-old girl asked who the visitor had been, and when Ms. Smith explained that the visitor had been her mother, the 10-year-old girl exclaimed, "YOU HAVE A MOTHER!"[42]

• TV and movie star Sarah Michelle Gellar got her start in TV commercials. As a very young child, she starred in a commercial for Burger King in which she criticized McDonald's hamburgers. McDonald's was so angered by the commercial that it sued lots of people connected with it, including five-year-old Sarah. She remembers once telling her friends, "I can't play," because she had to see some lawyers.[43]

• The very young son of writer Amy Hollingsworth learned nonviolent ways of dealing with anger. One day, when he was angry at her, he drew a picture of a smiley face, then he crossed it out and slipped it under her bedroom door. Later, after she had talked with him and he was no longer angry at her, he slipped two other pictures he had drawn under her door: a smiley face and a heart.[44]

• At age 13, ballet dancer Yvette Chauviré visited her grandmother in the country. Outside on a nice summer day, she danced, making up her own ballet. The next day, her grandmother overheard two women gossiping about young Yvette: "You didn't see? The granddaughter of Mme. Chauviré? But that child is insane! Poor little girl, so young, and already crazy!"[45]

• As a child, Hugh McIlhenny, aka "The King," developed his incredible ability to run with the football. His mother used to send him to go to the store, and to get to the store, he had to go through a scary dark alley. Whenever he had to go through the alley, he ran as fast as he could to escape the dangers he thought were lurking hidden in the shadows.[46]

• The creativity of young children can be amazing. Jean Little, the author of *Little by Little*, had an aunt named Ruth whose family had been too poor to buy her a doll when she was a young girl. Therefore, she had pretended that three kitchen chairs were dolls. She dressed them with rags, played with them, and even talked to them.[47]

• Sometimes, young people don't have their priorities set properly. In the 1940s, Ilene Beckerman used to make sure that she was wearing perfume and mascara before going to her class at Ballet Arts in the Carnegie Building in New York City — but her mother would yell at her because she had forgotten to wash her neck.[48]

• The four-year-old daughter of a friend of writer Carol Tavris took a bath with a very young male cousin, during which she made an interesting anatomical discovery. That night, as her mother was tucking her into bed, the four-year-old girl said, "Mommy, isn't it a blessing he doesn't have it on his face?"[49]

• Mikaela, the daughter of movie director Steven Spielberg, saw her father on television for the very first time in 1996 when he appeared on the Academy Awards show. Mikaela's mother held her in front of the TV and told her, "Look, honey, there's your daddy." She burped.[50]

• When Olympic gold-medal-winning gymnast Kerri Strug was a small child, her "gym" at home was a carpeted room that was temporarily without furniture. She spent lots of time there walking on her hands, and when her parents put furniture in the room, she cried.[51]

• Nick Carter, the youngest Backstreet Boy, started entertaining at an early age. When he was a very small child, his mother caught him standing on a tree stump and entertaining an audience consisting entirely of flowers, so she decided to quickly enroll him in singing lessons.[52]

• Even as a young child, artist Andy Warhol was different. He once disappeared from a neighborhood baseball game, as the other players discovered when someone hit the baseball to where Andy was supposed to be. Later, John, his brother, found him drawing flowers.[53]

• Young people in love do silly things. When Mark Twain was five years old, he fell in love with Laura Hawkins, who was the model for Becky Thatcher in *The Adventures of Tom Sawyer*. Young Mark had an apple, and he so loved Laura that he gave her the apple core.[54]

• Growing up with two totally blind parents can lead to odd situations. For example, Etta Reid decided that 11-year-old Julie, her sighted daughter, needed a bra after feeling Julie's breasts. Back then, Julie was horribly embarrassed, but today she thinks it's funny.[55]

• Being a famous opera singer in the days before quick and easy travel was quite rough. After Ernestine Schumann-Heink came back home in Europe after spending her first year singing in America, Ferdinand, her little son, asked her, "Is your name Mama?"[56]

• In St. Paul's Lutheran Church in Onalaska, Wisconsin, Bill Bader gave a children's sermon on the proper use of time. At one point, he asked for examples of a waste of time, and a three-year-old girl said, "How about taking a bath?"[57]

Chapter 2: From Christmas to Education

Christmas

• When she was a young girl, children's book author Marion Dane Bauer was infuriated when her parents lied to her — as parents did at that time (the 1940s and early 1950s) when they didn't want their children to know about such things as divorce. For example, young Marion had not seen her godfather's wife for a long time, and so she asked about her. Her mother told her that her godfather had never had a wife. Because of such lies and the way they made her feel, Ms. Bauer has been very honest with her own children — in fact, her daughter tells her that she is "pathologically honest." For example, when her three-and-a-half-year-old son asked about Santa Claus and whether he had really put gifts in the stockings, she told him the truth. That was fine, but it had the unintended effect of never allowing her daughter, who was two years younger than her son, to believe in Santa Claus because her older brother told her the truth. Today, the daughter, a grown woman, usually tells the truth, but is not "pathological" about it.[58]

• In grade 5, young adult author Chris Crutcher got into trouble with a Christian teacher. It was almost Christmas, and the teacher had assigned the students the task of seeing how many words they could create from the phrase "Merry Christmas." The young student had written first "Chris," then "Christ" on his list. His teacher ordered him to change the list and put "Christ" first, then his name. Frequently rebellious, Chris refused, and the teacher said that when Chris put his own name before the name Christ, he was committing the sin of pride.[59]

• Many very young children don't realize that what happens on stage is not real. At Christmas, Ernestine Schumann-Heink played the role of the Witch in the opera *Hansel and Gretel* while her children were very small, and when her character was put in the oven, her young son Ferdinand cried out, "They're putting my mother in the oven and burning her up!" Fortunately, Ms. Schumann-Heink came out of the other side of the oven quickly, and little Ferdinand saw that she was all right.[60]

• Tennis star Arthur Ashe valued education. When Camera, his daughter (her mother and his wife was the photographer Jeanne Moutoussamy), read to him for the first time a whole book out loud, he cried. Camera was raised well — each Christmas her father would take her to visit less fortunate families, to whose children they gave toys, including some that Camera had been given that day.[61]

• When escape artist Harry Houdini was a child, he worked as a messenger boy. One Christmas Eve, when his family was impoverished and lacked food, he came home from work and told his mother, "Shake me — I'm magic." He then shook himself, and coins fell on the floor — they were the tips he had collected that day. That Christmas, his family ate well.[62]

• One Christmas Eve, humorist Robert Benchley was having lunch with some friends at a restaurant, but he rose to go home. His friends urged him to stay a little longer, but he explained, "I owe it to the children — they've never seen me drunk." (By the way, Mr. Benchley was only joking — he was not drunk.)[63]

• When comedian Bill Hicks was very ill and showing signs of the pancreatic cancer that would kill him, he celebrated his final Christmas with his family, and Rachel, his seven-year-old niece, who had not been told that he was ill, turned to him and said, "Uncle Bill, you're going to be our first angel."[64]

• On December 13 in Hungary, girls write down on slips of paper the names of eligible bachelors, put them under their pillow, and draw out one name each day until Christmas, when only one name remains. According to folklore, that is the name of the boy they will marry.[65]

Clothing

• While attending high school in the 1950s, Ilene Beckerman and a friend each wanted a "basketball sweater" but unfortunately they lacked athlete boyfriends to give them sweaters — also unfortunately, their high school didn't have a basketball team. Eventually, Ilene and her friend discovered a store that would custom-make these sweaters — but only if a minimum of four sweaters was ordered. Therefore, Ilene, her friend, and two other girls ordered sweaters. On the back of the sweater was a space for the name of the team, but since the girls lacked a team they had "WC'WD" embroidered there. The initials stood for "We Couldn't Think of a Name, So We Didn't." (By the way, the girls were so young that they thought the salesman was "vulgar" when he measured their chests when they ordered the custom-made sweaters.)[66]

• Mary Moody Emerson, the aunt of Ralph Waldo Emerson, once was visited by the mother of Henry David Thoreau, author of *Walden*. Cynthia Thoreau was wearing clothing with pink ribbons, and Mary Emerson shut her eyes while talking to her. Eventually, she asked Mrs. Thoreau if she would like to know the reason for the tightly closed eyes. Mrs. Thoreau said that she would, and Mary Emerson replied, "I don't like to see a person of your age guilty of such levity in her dress."[67]

Comedians

• Phyllis Diller was an amateur comedian before she became a professional comedian. At college, she amused her female dorm mates by walking the halls with a rose in her mouth, a belt around her waist, curlers on her head, and nothing else. She also used to memorize jokes before going on dates. Later, as a homemaker before she became a professional comedian, she entertained other homemakers at the Laundromat.[68]

• The Three Stooges' Curly loved making children laugh. After suffering a stroke, he was forced to retire. Long-time Stooges short-film director Jules White visited him, and at one point, Curly got tears in his eyes and said to him, "I'm never going to make the children laugh again, am I, Jules?" (A few years after Curly died, the Three Stooges' short films started being shown on television and Curly again made children laugh.)[69]

• Some of the comedy routines of Mike Nichols and Elaine May started with a line from real life. For example, Mr. Nichols' mother once telephoned him and said, "Hello, Michael, this is your mother — do you remember me?" Mr. Nichols had to ask her to hang up so he could call Ms. May and tell her about the new comedy line they would improvise around that night.[70]

Couples

• Hugh Porter went through many girlfriends. One of his long-distance girlfriends, who didn't know that she had stopped being one of his girlfriends, telegraphed him, "Why don't you write?" Because Hugh was attending college, he sent back this telegram: "I am married to my Alma Mater." A few weeks passed, then a package arrived for him. The package contained a set of six silver teaspoons, and a note: "Best wishes to you and Alma for your happiness."[71]

• Even Hollywood celebrities have boyfriend trouble. Freddie Prinze, Jr., the boyfriend of Sarah Michelle Gellar, with whom he starred in the *Scoobie Doo* movies, was constantly late to his dates with her because he found it difficult to follow directions. To help solve that problem, she bought him a detailed map of Los Angeles. (By the way, they got married.)[72]

• Eleanor of Aquitaine picked lice from the hair of her lover and put it in a locket that she wore around her neck. Because she was royalty — the wife of King Louis VII of France — the women in her court imitated her and so she started a trend.[73]

• *New Yorker* cartoonist Alice Harvey loved roller-skating. In fact, when she received a big check from *The New Yorker*, she ordered built a circular sidewalk in her backyard just so she and her husband could roller-skate.[74]

Dance

• When ballerina Chan Hon Goh was a little girl, she took classes at her parents' dance school. One day, after class, when she was 13 years old, her parents began to talk about the accomplishments of some of the students in her classes. Feeling ignored, young Chan said, crying, "I was in all of those classes today, too. You never even notice. I don't know what the other girls have got that I don't. I try just as hard. How come you never correct me or praise me like you do the others?" Your father was surprised by her outburst, but he promised her, "If you really want to be a dancer, then I will work with you. I will watch you and correct you. Everything I can, I will do. From now on, I will take care of you." Both Chan and her father kept their word: she worked hard, and he corrected her. The hard work paid off — Chan became a prima ballerina with the National Ballet of Canada.[75]

• When the ballet *Rodeo* opened, it was a smash hit with the audience applauding for 22 curtain calls. Even the musicians in the orchestra pit were giving a standing ovation — a sure sign of success. Agnes de Mille, who choreographed the ballet and danced the part of the Cowgirl, was responsible for much of the ballet's success. An unsung hero was her mother, Anna, who supported Agnes through years of struggle. Asked if she was proud of her daughter after *Rodeo* had opened, Anna replied that she had always been proud of her daughter, including during the times when Agnes could find no one to give her work in dance.[76]

• When Alicia Martinez was attending ballet school in Cuba, the school suffered from a lack of male ballet dancers. Therefore, young Alicia asked her brother to round up a group of his friends and make them dance with her, promising them that she would teach them wonderful new exercises that would make them great athletes. One of the boys her brother rounded up was Fernando Alonso, whom Alicia later married.[77]

Death

• Occasionally, people use their wills to express disappointment with a loved one — or with someone who ought to be a loved one. For example, in her will the late Sara Clarke, from Bournemouth, England, wrote this: "To my daughter, I leave £1 — for the kindness and love she has never shown me." That is a recent example, but this kind of thing has been going on for a long time. The Earl of Stafford, in the late 1600s, wrote this in his will: "To the worst of women, Claude Charlotte de Grammont, unfortunately my wife, guilty as she is of all crimes, I leave five-and-forty brass halfpence, which will buy a pullet [a young hen] for her supper. A better gift than her father can make her; for I have known when having not the money, neither had he the credit for such a purchase; he being the worst of men, and his wife the worst of women in all debaucheries. Had I known their characters I had never married their daughter, and made myself unhappy." Here is one more example, again from England: "To the perfetic [pathetic] woman what was once my wife I leave the sum of 1p [pence] which she can shove up her arse."[78]

• Rich Moore, a member of the Crimson River Quartet in Mission Viejo, California, says that this story is true: A southern gospel group was asked by a widow to sing her husband's three favorite songs at his funeral; the songs were "In the Garden," "Amazing Grace," and "Jingle Bells." The members of the group were understandably leery of singing "Jingle Bells" at a funeral, but they did sing it — at a much slower tempo than usual. After they had sung the song, the widow said that she now remembered her husband's favorite song. It wasn't "Jingle Bells" — it was "When They Ring Those Golden Bells."[79]

• In the old days, before modern medicine developed, people had lots of children because they expected some of the children to die. They were knowledgeable about death, having seen it so often, and so they accepted it. Artist Grandma Moses had 10 children, but five died at birth or soon after. One daughter, Anna, collapsed during a Christmas party at age 37, and died a few days afterward. Before dying, she promised her daughter a birthday party. Grandma Moses first gave a funeral for her daughter, then gave a birthday party for her granddaughter.[80]

• John Weir was once inaccurately referred to as "the late John Weir" in the *New York Native*. Shortly afterward, he ran into a friend on the street, who was shocked to see that he was still alive. The friend asked him, "What are you doing on the planet? I thought you were dead." Mr. Weir assured him that he was still alive, and the friend, who was burdened with too many things to do and not enough time to do them, complained without thinking, "Now I'll have to put you back in my Rolodex."[81]

• In New England, a tourist saw an elderly man tending a ceremony. She asked him, "Do people often die in this town?" The elderly man gruffly replied, "No, they die only once." Trying again, the tourist asked him, "Do a lot of people die in this town?" The elderly man gruffly replied, "Yes, all of them do."[82]

• Johnny Carson's final show, "Funny Moments and a Final Farewell," was shown on May 22, 1992. The final image shown as he walked off the set at the end of the show was a photograph of a sunset. It was taken by Rick Carson, his son, who had died in an automobile accident in 1991.[83]

Education

• As a freshman in high school, Chris Crutcher, who is now an author of books for young adults, played a mean trick on the most unpopular girl in his class — he made her the freshman candidate for the Cascade High School Carnival Queen. Normally, of course, honors such as this go to the most popular girls at school, but Chris had a friend nominate the unpopular girl for Carnival Queen and he got all his friends to vote for her, and so she was the freshman candidate for Carnival Queen. Of course, the freshman class advisor realized what had happened, and he did not want the unpopular girl to be hurt by not having a date to the Carnival Dance and by being ignored at the

Carnival Dance, so he called a meeting of all the freshman boys and told them exactly what they were to do at the dance. First, each of the boys had to draw a number, and whichever boy drew the number 1 had to invite the unpopular girl to the dance. In addition, each boy had to dance three times with the unpopular girl, and he made it clear to each boy that any boy who danced only twice with her would regret it. (This was in the days when teachers were respected, when parents did not sue schools, and when corporal punishment was not only allowed but encouraged by everyone except the students.) At the dance, the boys did each dance three dances with the unpopular girl, and during one of the times that Chris was dancing with her, she told him, "I know this was a joke — but this is still the best night of my life." At the time, Chris realized only how cruel his joke had been. Much later, he felt admiration for this teenage girl who had had a cruel joke played on her but had still managed to turn it into something good.[84]

• When he was very small, children's book author and artist Tomie dePaola desperately wanted to learn to read. In fact, he almost decided not to attend kindergarten when he learned that he wouldn't be taught to read until the first grade — he attended kindergarten only after being told that he had to in order to be admitted to the first grade. Unfortunately, his first-grade book wasn't very exciting. It was filled with sentences such as these: "See Dick run. Run, Dick, run. Run, run, run." The kind of book that young Tomie wanted to learn to read began with sentences such as this: "Once upon a time, in a deep dark wood stood the cottage of the woodcutter." But he needed to learn to read because only then could he get a library card, and so he took the book home that Friday without permission. Because he had "stolen" the book, his mother made him confess his misdeed and apologize to the teacher the following Monday. But then a wonderful thing happened. Tomie had learned to read the book over the weekend, and he read it to his teacher. She was so impressed that she gave him a library card, and Tomie was on his way to reading books that began with sentences such as this: "Once upon a time, in a deep dark wood stood the cottage of the woodcutter."[85]

• You don't have to be a Ph.D. to be a "professor." When African-American (and world-class) artist Jacob Lawrence was growing up in Harlem in the first half of the 20th century — a time when white educators mostly ignored African-American history, African-American biography, and African-American heroes — he became interested in his heritage. People told him to go to the lectures of Professor Seyfert. Mr. Seyfert, an African-American, earned his education through reading books, not through attending college lectures, and he earned his money through working as a carpenter. Eager to share his knowledge, he gave exciting lectures about African-American accomplishments wherever he could: the YMCA, the public library on 135th Street, etc. Later, Mr. Lawrence created many works of art about such African-American heroes as Harriet Tubman and General Toussaint L'Ouverture.[86]

• Shammai and Hillel were both great Jewish teachers, but only Hillel had patience. A non-Jew came to see Shammai. The non-Jew pointed to the students in the room and said, "I do not have time to study your laws, your Torah, everyday like these students, but I would like to become a Jew if you can teach me the entire Torah while I stand on one foot." Shammai sent the non-Jew away, saying, "You expect to learn in one minute what these men study their entire lives? That is impossible." So the non-Jew went to Hillel and made the same request. Hillel listened carefully to the non-Jew, then said, "That which you hate, do not do to your neighbor. That is the whole Torah. All the rest is explanation and commentary. Now learn the rest so you will truly understand what I have just taught you." The non-Jew became both a Jew and a devoted student.[87]

• Richard P. Feynman, a Nobel Prize winner in Physics in 1965, reviewed science and mathematics textbooks for the California State Curriculum Committee, pointing out both what was good and what was bad in textbooks that were being considered for use in California schools. He was concerned about bright children, and he did not want bright children to be penalized for solving problems in ways not discussed in the teachers' manuals that came with the textbooks. In fact, his daughter Michelle was penalized for solving an algebra problem in a way not covered by the teachers' manual. Mr. Feynman spoke to Michelle's teacher, who told him that he (Mr. Feynman) didn't understand mathematics! Following this confrontation between teacher and parent, Michelle studied algebra at home. She went to school only to take the required tests.[88]

• An impoverished young man who worked as a water carrier in Jerusalem saw a beautiful young woman — the daughter of a rich man — and fell in love with her. He asked her to marry him, but although she was attracted to him, she replied, "Do you know who my father is? Me marry a water carrier? He'd fall over, laughing." The young man decided to become more than a mere water carrier, so he began attending school with very young children, learning the Hebrew alphabet with them, and he began his study of religious texts. Eventually, he became the well-educated, great Rabbi Akiba, and he married the beautiful young woman.[89]

• A Monsignor was both overweight and the superintendent of some Catholic schools. One day, he sat in on a first-grade classroom where the Sister teaching the class was reading the children a story about a pony. After reading the story, the Sister asked the children if they thought the Monsignor had ever ridden a pony. The children all answered, "No," but the Monsignor explained that he had ridden a pony when he was young. One little boy, unfortunately, said, "But you couldn't ride one now, because you'd squash the poor pony." Fortunately — and to the relief of the Sister — the Monsignor laughed.[90]

• According to NBA superstar Larry Bird, speaking in an interview with Tom Callahan, "The guy who won't do his schoolwork misses the free throw at the end." He and most of the other members of his high-school basketball team would practice shooting free throws at 6:30 a.m. before school started. One player, however, never showed up. Tournament time came, and that player missed the front end of three one-and-ones in a row during the regional finals. His — and Bird's — team lost in overtime. Mr. Bird says, "I never said nothing to him. I just looked at him, and he knew."[91]

• Arlene Istar Lev, LCSW, CASAC, author of *How Queer: Lesbian, Gay, Bisexual and Transgender Parenting*, once watched a young boy do his homework: writing short sentences to describe the pictures on a worksheet. For a picture showing two short-haired children playing together, he wrote, "The boys are playing." Ms. Lev asked him how he knew the two short-haired children were boys. He replied, "Because they don't have dykes in school." He was a smart boy. In his home life, he knew short-haired females, but he also knew that in school-worksheet pictures, girls always had long hair.[92]

• Danny, the computer scientist brother of young people's author William Sleator, had a hard time learning to read when he was a young child. One day, he went with his father to his father's lab. Left alone for a short time, he studied a fire alarm on the wall and deciphered the word PULL. Having deciphered the word, he then followed the instructions and pulled, setting off the fire alarm. His father was not upset; instead, he was happy that Danny was finally showing signs that he was not illiterate.[93]

• The grandmother of young adult author Chris Crutcher used to tell him a story about when his father was a boy. In the sixth grade, he came home and told her, "A lot of the other kids in my class think I'm arrogant." She told him that he could change the other kids' opinion of him by doing such things as not answering every question the teacher asked and letting the other kids have a chance to answer a few questions. Chris' father thought for a moment, then said, "Naw, I'd rather be arrogant."[94]

• The pupils of a teacher wished to drive evil from the world, so they asked him how to do that. The teacher took his pupils to a dark basement and told them that they would drive the darkness from the basement. First, the teacher told his pupils to use sticks to beat the darkness out of the basement, but that didn't work. Next, the teacher told his pupils to shout at and curse the darkness to drive it out of the basement, but that didn't work. Finally, the teacher told his pupils to light a candle.[95]

• Many students are afraid of being made uncomfortable in the classroom because of exposure to beliefs that are different from their own. Writer Anna Quindlen once asked Elizabeth Castelli, a professor of religion at Barnard College, if she did anything to keep her students from feeling uncomfortable in the classroom. She replied, "It is not my job to make people comfortable. It is [my job] to educate them." Ms. Quindlen wrote that when she heard this, "I nearly stood up and cheered."[96]

• Following the 9-11 attack on the World Trade Center, many Americans wanted revenge. A week after the attack, Dean Dorothy Denburg of Barnard College saw many people wearing Barnard College T-shirts on Fifth Avenue in New York passing out leaflets that called for tolerance toward people of all religions and all backgrounds. This took courage as many, many people, including high-ranking American politicians, wanted war, even against a country that had nothing to do with 9-11.[97]

• Not everyone supports giving honorary degrees to celebrities, including royal celebrities. In 1986, Monash University gave Prince Philip an honorary science degree. To protest, the Monash Association of Students gave their own honorary degree — to a 21-month-old Chihuahua. Some people thought the Chihuahua deserved the honorary degree as much as the prince did. Other people disagree, saying that the Chihuahua deserved the honorary degree more than the prince did.[98]

• At times, students become excited by learning. During Spring Quarter of 1970, Ohio University professor Robert DeMott offered a course titled "Writers of the Beat Movement." The course drew so many students that there was standing room only, with many students spilling out of the classroom and into the hallway. Later in 1970, he taught an Honors course on beat poet Gary Snyder — the class met in a teepee on property owned by an Ohio University art professor.[99]

• Many books for young people have been censored or challenged, although defenders of free speech have often stood up to the would-be censors. For example, a librarian in the New York City school system threatened to quit if Paul Zindel's novel *The Pigman* were placed in the library. Her supervisors told her to quit — if students wanted to read *The Pigman*, they could.[100]

• Actor Will Smith's father was strongly against illegal drugs. When Will was a teenager, his father drove him around the poorer sections of Philadelphia, showing him bums with nowhere to sleep but doorways. He told Will, "This is what people look like when they do drugs." Will says, "I never tried drugs because I felt he would kill me. Literally."[101]

• In one of her classes, Marcia Worth-Baker decided to involve her students in an activity in which they put the ancient Greek god Zeus, god of lightning, on trial. However, the student playing Pandora, the prosecutor, got a lot of laughs when she announced that Zeus' crimes included cutting in line and reading other people's e-mail.[102]

• As a kid, Indiana basketball coach Bobby Knight understood the value of reading. In his hometown of Orrville, Ohio, the library posted a list of the 10 kids in town who had read the most books that week. Each week, young Bobby's name was on that list — along with the names of nine girls.[103]

• At the end of her second day in school, a first-grade student asked her teacher, "What did I do in school today?" Surprised, the teacher asked why the student had asked that. The student replied,

"Well, I'm going home now, and when I get home, my mother will ask me that."[104]

• Some people are born teachers. Las Vegas elementary-schoolteacher Ainslie Cole started teaching when she was a little girl — she taught her very first math lesson to a room filled with very special students: her stuffed animals.[105]

• At a very young age, comedian Bill Hicks liked Elvis Presley. When Bill was in first grade, he lip-synched "All Shook Up" at school — on the teacher's desk — for show and tell.[106]

• Christian Johannsen was an exacting teacher of ballet. When he wished to give high praise to a student, he would tell him or her, "Now you may do that in public."[107]

Chapter 3: From Fathers to Homes

Fathers

• Actor Will Smith learned a lot from his father while growing up in Philadelphia, PA. When Will was still in school, his father ordered him and his brother, Harry, to replace — brick by brick — a wall in their yard. Will couldn't believe it because the wall was about 16 feet high and about 50 feet wide. He says, "I remember standing there thinking, 'There is no way I will live to see this completed.' He wanted us to build the Great Wall of Philly! I remember hoping that my father would get committed, because if he were in an insane asylum, then we wouldn't have to finish the thing." The wall took six months to rebuild, including mixing the concrete by hand. Of course, Will and Harry — and their father — were proud of their work when it was done. Today Will says, "Dad told me and my brother, 'Now don't you all ever tell me you can't do something.' I look back on that a lot of times in my life when I think I won't be able to do something, and I tell myself, 'One brick at a time.'"[108]

• When children's mystery writer Joan Lowery Nixon was a child, she studied arithmetic, but often ran into difficult problems. Her father was an accountant, and he would explain the process of solving the problems, and she would then do her homework. However, occasionally one or two problems were very difficult, and her father would not tell her how to solve them. Instead, he would tell her, "Think about them when you go to bed. Tell your mind to work on them. It will do this while you're asleep. In the morning, when you wake up, you'll be able to solve the problems." Later, Ms. Lowery read books about the subconscious, and she told her father, "You were way ahead of your time." Her father laughed and replied, "It wasn't my idea. My second-grade teacher taught the process to me."[109]

• Both Lillian Moller Gilbreth and Frank Bunker Gilbreth were efficiency experts; indeed, Mr. Gilbreth invented the field and applied it to his personal life and the life of his family. Mr. Gilbreth even attempted to save time by shaving with two razors. (He had already cut — perhaps an unfortunate choice of words — 17 seconds from his shaving time by lathering his face with two brushes.) Unfortunately, Mr. Gilbreth cut himself with one of the razors and had to waste two minutes bandaging himself up. According to his children, "It wasn't the slashed throat that really bothered him. It was the two minutes."[110]

• Elite gymnast Kerri Strug was badly injured at a meet at which her father was present. Someone told her father, "Dr. Strug, don't worry. She'll be fine for the U.S. Championships." Dr. Strug got mad and replied, "I don't care about any gymnastics meet or anything but Kerri right now. I don't care if she ever walks into a gym again. I want to know if she's ever going to be able to walk. I want to know if she's ever going to be able to have children and hold her children in her arms." Fortunately, Ms. Strug did recover with no ill effects — and she won a team gold medal at the 1996 Olympics in Atlanta.[111]

• Bob Newhart was a family man as well as a comedian and a comic actor. While making *The Bob Newhart Show,* he owned a very large watch instead of one of the small digital watches that were then becoming popular. When Oliver Clark, who played Mr. Herd on the sitcom, asked why he had bought such a large watch, Mr. Newhart replied that around 3 or 4 p.m. he would take a look at his watch, very obviously and very significantly, to let the people around him know that he was ready to go home and see his children. For that particular purpose, he needed a big watch.[112]

• After lesbian comedian Kate Clinton came out to her father (he was good about it — he told her that he wanted her to be happy, to be safe, and to get health insurance), she invited him to dinner with her and some of her lesbian friends. No topics for discussion were off limits, except for one. For her own comfort, she told her friends not to talk about sex. Near the end of the meal, one of her friends asked her father, "Well, Mr. Clinton, what do you think we as gay people can do to make more bridges to straight people?" Her father replied, "Keep talking."[113]

• Financial writer Andrew Tobias knows two very intelligent gay parents. One father is American; the other father is French. That means that their two daughters are growing up bilingual in English and French. In addition, their housekeeper is Spanish and the only TV the two daughters were allowed to watch when they were younger was Spanish-language Disney tapes. The result: the girls are trilingual. By the way, the two girls were shocked when they visited a young friend. They came home and shouted, "Daddy! Papa! Penelope's TV speaks English!"[114]

• Golfer Peter Jacobsen's voice was used in the game Golden Tee Golf, which was very popular in bars. One day, Mr. Jacobsen's two daughters, Kristen and Amy, were in a bar. Both were college students, both were underage, and both were using fake IDs to buy alcohol. Suddenly, they heard their father's voice saying, "It's great to be here." "Oh, my God!" Amy said. "Kristen, Dad's here!" Both daughters ducked under the bar table, hoping that their father had not seen them, then discovered that they were sitting next to a Golden Tee game.[115]

• Christy Hauptman started skydiving as a teenager, but she had a rocky — and terrified — start. Her father took her up in an airplane, and she was supposed to jump out at 15,000 feet. Instead, she started cursing and screamed at her father, "There's no way I'm stepping out of this plane! I'll die if I do!" (Many expletives have been deleted from that quotation.) This was the first time she had ever cursed that much — especially in front of her father. However, she decided to jump, she enjoyed it, and she has jumped hundreds of times since then.[116]

• When Makeda Zook was in the third grade, a class project was to make a Father's Day card. However, young Makeda had two lesbian mothers — her father was a sperm donor. Knowing this, her teacher asked her for which male in her life she would like to make a Father's Day card. The choice was difficult — she could make a Father's Day card for either her late grandfather, or for her guinea pig, which was a male. In the end, the card was gifted to Chocolate the guinea pig.[117]

• Burt Strug met his future wife, Melanie, one summer. Within one month he had convinced her to transfer to his college — and within three months he had convinced her to marry him. Today, he tells their daughter, elite gymnast Kerri Strug, "If you ever do something that dumb for a boy, I'll strangle you."[118]

• Tito Fuentes, a major-league infielder, disliked knock-down pitches for what may — or may not — be a very good reason: "They shouldn't throw at me. I'm the father of five or six kids."[119]

Food

• William M. Gaines, the publisher of *MAD* magazine, loved food — and lots of it. One day, he treated the staff to a meal at the Gotham Bar and Grill, and when he ordered, he ordered LOTS of food. In fact, the number of entrees ordered at a *MAD* dinner usually numbered twice the number of diners. For one thing, Mr. Gaines would order a few entrees for himself only, as well as a few that were simply placed on the table so that anyone could help himself if he were so inclined. On this occasion, he and his staff ordered so many appetizers, entrees, desserts, and wines that a waitress appeared on an errand from the kitchen. "The chef sent me out," she said. "He wants to know, Who *are* you?" On one occasion, the wait staff brought over an additional table — not for extra diners, but simply to have room for all the food and drink that had been ordered. (This occasion turned into a four-hour feeding frenzy.) *MAD* writer Dick DeBartolo was a dessert freak, and at his first meal with Mr. Gaines, he told him that he always looked at the dessert menu first, so he would know whether to order a heavy or a light entree. Mr. Gaines said to order whatever he wanted for the entree and let him take care of dessert. When it was time for dessert, Mr. Gaines ordered one of every choice, so the waiter brought over an entire dessert cart and left it.[120]

• When figure skater Sasha Cohen was a little girl, her parents would not let her eat junk food at home, so she had to get spoiled at her grandparents' house. She remembers her grandmother's brand of discipline: "Sasha, you cannot have ice cream if you do not finish your doughnut first!" Sasha was a lover of ice cream, even at age 5, so she loved her grandmother's other strict rule: No child is allowed to eat ice cream more than three times per day. Her parents would sometimes indulge her with a kid's ice cream cone away from the house, and Sasha remembers once requesting of the salesperson, "Please make my kid's cone extra large." He thought that this was funny, and so the scoop that he gave her was huge. She once ordered ice cream in a cup at a restaurant, but the server forgot to bring her a spoon. No problem. Young Sasha knew that spoons were located in a big container nearby, so she went to the container, which was high above her head, and she started pulling on it. Soon, the container and lots of silverware tumbled noisily to the ground. Everyone in the restaurant grew quiet, but little Sasha triumphantly held a spoon up and announced, "I got it!" The people in the restaurant applauded.[121]

• Queen Kaahumanu was the first feminist of Hawaii. When she was born, women on the islands had to live by many rules. For example, women were not allowed to eat with the men, and women were not allowed to eat bananas, or pork, or coconuts, or baked dog. However, when her husband, King Kamehameda, died, Queen Kaahumanu decided to make a few changes. First, she became the joint ruler of the islands, along with Liholiho, her husband's son by another wife. Then she and Liholiho's mother started to change society by doing such things as eating bananas in front of the new king. The new king was open to the changes, and soon, the new king started eating at the same table with them. The Hawaiian people also welcomed the changes and made great changes in their way of living, including destroying many wooden idols.[122]

• When David B. Feinberg got AIDS, he had to make changes to his diet. For example, he was advised to put on extra pounds while he still could because AIDS wastes away the body. Also, he had to avoid such foods as sushi and soft, runny cheeses — such as brie. This upset Mr. Feinberg. He complained to a friend named John Palmer Weir, Jr., "How can I be a card-carrying homo without brie?" Mr. Weir pointed out, "There's still quiche. We'll always have quiche."[123]

• Arturo Toscanini and Carla, his wife, once visited the home of Arthur O'Connell. Mrs. Toscanini, always a curious sort, went into the kitchen to investigate a huge pot of spaghetti. The Italian cook, always a sensitive sort, abandoned the kitchen to ask Mr. O'Connell who "that woman" was. Fortunately, the cook was pleased to learn that "that woman" was Mrs. Toscanini, and fortunately, the spaghetti was excellent and enjoyed by all.[124]

• While in Paris, Robert Benchley told some friends that he had once had some memorable pressed duck in a restaurant in Montmartre, so they all set off for the restaurant. Unfortunately, after everyone had ordered and been served the pressed duck, Mr. Benchley recalled why the pressed duck was so memorable — it was the worst he had ever tried to eat.[125]

• During Lent, many Christians give up something they like as a sign of penitence. One small boy gave up ice cream — "all except chocolate."[126]

Games and Contests

• Young people's novelist William Sleator grew up in a family of oddballs. When William was a young boy, his father, his younger sister Vicky, and he used to play a game. His father would blindfold them, drive them to a part of the city that William and Vicky had never been before, then drop them off and let them find their way back home. Of course, William and Vicky did have enough money to call home in case they ran into trouble finding their way back. The only time they used the telephone money was when two of their friends came along to play the game and panicked. Then William and Vicky let their friends use the money to call their home. Unfortunately, since the two friends didn't know where they were in the city, they also panicked their parents, who called Mr. Sleator. Mr. Sleator calmly finished his lunch, which he had just started eating, then drove off and found the children within 10 minutes. Meanwhile, the friends' parents called the police, and both parents left the house to look for the children. Mr. Sleator did not know the police had been called, and he could not contact the friends' parents, since they had both left home. (This was in the days before cell phones.) Perhaps understandably, the friends thereafter did not visit the Sleators.[127]

• When Marvel Comics maven Stan Lee was fifteen years old, he started entering a news contest run by the *New York Herald-Tribune*. Contestants were supposed to write in 500 words or fewer their pick for the top news story of the week. Mr. Lee entered the contest three times in a row, he won three times in a row, and the editor of the *Herald-Tribune* wrote him, saying to stop entering the contest so someone else could win for a change.[128]

Gifts

• When soprano Beverly Sills was a girl, she sang on Major Bowes' radio broadcasts. During one broadcast, Major Bowes said that he had given young Beverly a gift for good luck: a small figurine of an elephant. In the days following, Beverly received through the mail gifts of hundreds of small figurines of elephants. Beverly was intelligent. She mentioned on the air that she was upset because her mother wouldn't let her have long dresses. Sure enough, dozens of gifts of long dresses arrived in the mail for Beverly. She continued to con the audience by mentioning occasionally that she liked such items as Mickey Mouse watches and sleds.[129]

• When children's book author Sid Fleischman started going bald, his kids made him a hairpiece — they clipped hair from the family pet dog and glued it to fabric. Mr. Fleischman writes in his autobiography,

The Abracadabra Kid, that he was very happy with the gift — "It gave me a punk pompadour decades before spiked hairdos became trendy."[130]

• Dr. Barry Herman, a school principal in New Haven, Connecticut, once bought candy for an ill teacher, then presented it to her, saying, "Something sweet for a sweet person." Unfortunately, he had bought the candy at random, not bothering to read the label, which said, "Sour balls."[131]

Good Deeds

• Meredith Mendelson went to sea with Ocean Classroom when she was in high school. She worked hard both mentally and physically — going to sleep was no problem because she was so tired. One of the highlights of the trip was seeing a pod of humpback whales circling their ship. Unfortunately, this peaceful, quiet scene was ruined when several whale-watching boats came out from shore carrying tourists who wanted to see the whales. Their oohs, aahs, and other noises drove the whales away, as did their motors and diesel fuel. The tourists ruined the intimacy of the encounter with the whales for the sailors of Ocean Classroom. By the way, sometimes whales become entangled in nets and flotation devices left behind by fishermen, leading to death. In 2005 in Gordon's Bag, South Africa, police diver Eben Lourens cut away most of the ropes entangling a southern right whale. National Sea Rescue Institute Gordon's Bay Station Commander Stuart Burgess said, "We slowly approached [the whale] until we were about 30m away and then cut the engines. The whale swam up and gently bumped our rescue boat. At that point we got good visuals of the problem." He added, "We could see the ropes and buoys entangled around the tail and the pieces trailing behind her." Mr. Lourens was deployed ahead of the whale, and as the whale swam past him, he grabbed onto the fishing net and started cutting the ropes. He cut away most of the ropes and all of the flotation devices. Mr. Stuart said, "Although there is still some rope attached to the whale, we were unable to do more and we suspect that the remaining rope will fall free as it untangles." Mr. Lourens said, "It's not something I'd done before, so the adrenalin was pumping through me. But it was very satisfying afterwards." After the rescue, the whale was swimming much more easily. Mr. Burgess said that commercial crayfishers often left their nets behind: "We find them all the time. In one afternoon recently we found four of them." The nets are hazardous not only for whales, he said, but also for boats — especially at night. Freeing a whale can be very dangerous — even deadly — work. Nan Rice of the Save the Whales Campaign said, "It is very dangerous to attempt such a thing without the proper equipment and tools. The public must take note and not try and do this by themselves. You cannot swim up to a whale and try to cut it loose. It is extremely dangerous." In New Zealand, a diver was killed during an attempted whale rescue, she said: "The whale slammed its tail down on top of him, and he was gone. I feel that human lives are just as valuable as those of animals, and I don't think it is right to risk one for the other."[132]

• Civilians suffer during war, including the American Civil War. A hungry Virginian woman appeared at the Union camp of General Newton M. Curtis, asking for help. However, she was required to take an oath of allegiance to the Union cause before receiving food or other help. This she declined to do because both her husband and her son were fighting for the Confederate cause. Rather than letting her depart without help, General Curtis gave her money from his own pocket so she could buy food and other necessities.[133]

• In July 1863, a 16-year-old Confederate woman named Cornelia Barrett did a remarkable good deed for a dying Yankee soldier. He requested that she write a letter for him to his fiancée. He also requested that she send his fiancée a lock of his hair and his gold ring. She did as he asked, and a few months later she received a letter from the soldier's sweetheart, thanking her for her kindness.[134]

Grandparents

• The grandparents of children's book writer Phyllis Reynolds Naylor were characters. She called her paternal grandparents Pappaw and Mammaw. They began courting when she was an infant, and he was a little boy. He would pick her up and say, "This is the girl I'm going to marry." They did marry — when Mammaw was 15 years old and still playing with dolls. In contrast, her maternal grandparents were adults when they began to court. Her grandfather sent her grandmother a letter, asking two weeks in advance if he could go with her to church. He also offered to have a prominent doctor send a letter to her father stating that the man who wished to court his daughter had a good character.[135]

• The grandfather of Christian writer Dale Hanson Bourke was quite a lively and feisty character. One day, as he was driving during rush hour, a large bus edged him out of the lane he was driving in. This made Grandpa angry, so he rolled down his window and shouted at the bus driver to get out of his lane. The bus driver refused, saying that his bus was bigger than Grandpa's car. Therefore, Grandpa reached for a sledgehammer he was hauling in his car, hammered a large dent in the side of the bus, then drove off. Grandpa was also a mighty evangelizer — sometimes he even grabbed people by the lapels of their clothing and asked them, "Are you saved?"[136]

• When Grandma Moses at age 80 was invited to attend her first important one-person art exhibit at the Galerie St. Etienne in New York City, she declined to go. Why? As she explained to the gallery director, Otto Kallir, she had no reason to go — she had already seen all of the paintings. Shortly afterward, she did attend an exhibition of her paintings at a Gimbel Brothers department store in New York City. She brought some of her homemade bread and preserves, reasoning that since she had won prizes for them and not her paintings at the county fair, people would be asking her about food and not about art.[137]

• TV's Mister Rogers was a rambunctious kid. Whenever he was attempting to walk on a stone wall at his grandparents' farm and his mother or grandmother would try to stop him, his grandfather, who was named Fred McFeely, would tell them, "Let the kid walk on the wall. He's got to learn to do things for himself." Mister Rogers loved his grandfather, and in his TV "neighborhood," one of the characters was a lively old deliveryman named Mr. McFeely.[138]

• When the young granddaughter of artist Edna Hibel developed "lazy eye" and had to wear an eye patch under her glasses, Ms. Hibel taped over one lens of her glasses and painted a rose on it as a decoration to make wearing the eye patch a more pleasurable experience.[139]

Halloween

• Joe, the young son of Lisa M. Wayman, RN, started chemotherapy to treat his cancer, and his hair fell out. Therefore, for his Halloween costume, he dressed up as his bald father. Young Joe even wore a fake beard. Before he died, he taught his mother not to be so serious all the time and to laugh occasionally.[140]

Homes

• Many families have a hard time sharing a bathroom, which is sometimes the busiest room in a house. However, when Paris Singer of the family that manufactured Singer sewing machines bought modern dance pioneer Isadora Duncan a hotel outside Paris to serve as her dancing school, she didn't have to worry about that problem. Of the hotel's 200 rooms, 80 were bathrooms![141]

• Not all volcanic eruptions are swift. In Hawaii, one volcano emitted molten lava slowly. In fact, residents on the island had plenty of time to leave their houses and move their household possessions out of the line of lava. In some cases, people sat on lawn chairs and drank cold beer from a safe distance as they watched the molten lava flow upon and destroy their houses.[142]

Chapter 4: From Husbands and Wives to Music

Husbands and Wives

• *MAD* magazine publisher William M. Gaines met his wife, Annie, through the mail. As a sophomore at Penn State, she was assigned a project on pollution, and she wanted an article on pollution that had appeared in *MAD* magazine. Unable to find it in her personal collection (she was a *MAD* fan), she sent a dollar bill to the offices of *MAD* and requested a copy of the article. Mr. Gaines sent her a note saying, "Never send cash through the mail," and he enclosed both a check for $1 and an offer to send her the article for free — as long as she sent him a photograph of herself. She sent him a *Playboy* centerfold along with a detailed list of ways in which she did *not* resemble the centerfold model. Sometime later, they met in person and liked each other. (Things really got serious when Mr. Gaines met an ex-boyfriend of hers and noticed that the ex-boyfriend was heavy, like him.)[143]

• When American realist painter Andrew Wyeth proposed to Betsy James, she accepted immediately. Later, she said, "I knew at some point somebody was going to find me and know what I was all about. And it happened. Just like that. Boom!" Betsy was responsible for making Andrew independent of the instruction of his father, the eminent illustrator N.C. Wyeth. One day, she saw the two men together with an illustration of an Indian head that Andrew was creating for a book jacket. N.C. was touching up the illustration. Enraged, she left the room, slamming the door behind her. Thereafter, N.C. left his son's artwork alone.[144]

• Gymnasts can have more than one dream. In 1974, Joan Moore seemed poised to become the United States' first woman gymnast to win an Olympic medal. At the United States Elite Nationals in 1971, she tied for first in the all-around competition with Linda Matheny.

In 1972, she tied for first with Cathy Rigby. In 1973 and 1974, she won with no ties. However, in late 1974, she gave up the dream of an Olympic medal for a dream that was also important to her. She gave up her amateur status and Olympic eligibility so that she and her then-husband, Bob Rice, could open a gymnastics school in Minnesota.[145]

• Insult comedian Don Rickles is much different off stage than he is on. When he first met Bob Newhart's wife, Ginny, he talked about how much he loved his one-year-old daughter, who was named Mindy, and how much he hated being separated from her when he was on the road performing. After Mr. Rickles had left, Ginny told Bob, "That is the most darling man I've ever met. You just want to hug him." A little later, they caught Mr. Rickles' act, in which he told the audience, "Ladies and gentlemen, Bob Newhart is here with his wife, a former hooker from Bayonne, New Jersey." (Despite this beginning, they all became friends and have traveled the world together.)[146]

• Married couples get divorced for different reasons. Early 20th-century cartoonist Rose Cecil O'Neill was divorced twice in an era when that was very unusual and very suspect. One of her divorces resulted from her habit of speaking baby talk. However, despite this habit she was very capable of producing serious work. One of her cartoons — on a postcard — was titled "Give Mother the Vote: We Need It" and showed her usual cute, cuddly cartoon characters with this verse underneath the cartoon: "Isn't it a funny thing / That father cannot see / Why Mother ought to have a vote / On how these things should be?"[147]

• After working at the Disney studio, animator John Sibley stopped for a drink. One drink led to another, and he arrived home late — very late. However, his loving wife was waiting for him. She was dressed very elegantly, made up very beautifully, and had been eagerly looking forward to her husband's taking her out to dine and dance — as he had promised. (It was their wedding anniversary.) Mr. Sibley recognized his error, but being never at a loss for humorous words, he asked her, "What's new?" Of course, his loving wife forgave him, but it took time. (Three years.)[148]

• A woman who owned many slaves asked Rabbi Joshua what God had been doing since He created the universe. Rabbi Joshua answered that God had been busy pairing people into couples: husband and wife. The woman thought that she could do that as well as God, so she paired her slaves into couples, man and woman, and she made them get married. The next day, the slaves were in bad shape because of the fights that they had had, so she decided that she had better let God pair people into couples in the future.[149]

• Soprano Helen Traubel married too early, fell in love with another man, and divorced her husband so she could marry the other man. While visiting her native St. Louis, she met her first husband in the street. He asked her, "What do you remember of our marriage, Helen?" She replied, honestly, "I have a very pleasant memory of being married to a wonderful young man." He then said, "Yes, but we're all older now, aren't we?" They shook hands, and that was the last time they met.[150]

• Rabbi Yosef Chayim Sonnenfeld was once asked if it was OK to have a hot drink before saying the morning prayers. He replied that it was OK. Someone who knew the good rabbi well pointed out that he never had a hot drink before morning prayers. Rabbi Yosef replied, "You are right, but I don't for a special reason. I am afraid that if I have a hot drink before morning prayers, my wife might wake up early in the morning to warm the water for me." (At the time, that took considerable effort, including making a fire.)[151]

• Jerry Spinelli, author of *Stargirl*, a young people's novel about a free spirit, met his wife, Eileen Mesi, when she left a chocolate Easter bunny on his desk. (They worked at the same place.) Ms. Mesi carried around loose-leaf binders filled with her poetry, which she made him read. Not surprisingly, Ms. Mesi was the real-life model for Stargirl (the lead character in Mr. Spinelli's novel *Stargirl*) — and today she is a published author.[152]

• Connie Small, born 1898, was a lighthouse keeper's wife when lighthouses weren't automated with electricity. Instead, they were lit with kerosene, and it took 20 minutes to light a lighthouse. One lighthouse she and her husband stayed at was in New England, and sometimes she saw no one but her husband for four months at a time.[153]

• An actress' body is her instrument. Early in their marriage, Mel Brooks touched Anne Bancroft during an argument. She immediately drew herself up and said haughtily, "Don't you dare touch my instrument!" Mr. Brooks said, "Oh, so this is your instrument?" "Yes," she replied. "This is my instrument." "OK," said Mr. Brooks. "Play 'Melancholy Baby.'"[154]

• Early in the 20th century, Annie Reel, born 1893, met William Cogburn who was a police officer in Asheville, North Carolina. Mr. Cogburn asked her to marry him, but she replied, "Well, everyone wants to get married. But I don't want to get married without a house." So, she says, Mr. Cogburn built her a house, and "then I had to get married."[155]

• Flemish painter Peter Bruegel married a woman who lied a lot. Before he married her, they agreed that every time she lied Mr. Bruegel would notch a stick, and they agreed that when the stick was notched from top to bottom, then the marriage would be over. Mr. Bruegel used a very long stick, but the marriage was soon over.[156]

• Movie director Steven Spielberg says that in his second marriage — this time to actress Kate Capshaw — he understands that the rules of marriage say that he can't be a workaholic. According To Mr. Spielberg, "I perfectly understand the ground rules — 8:30 to 5:30 Monday to Friday is mine. Everything else is Kate's."[157]

• Pianist Anton Rubinstein liked to stay in bed much too late. Fortunately, his wife figured out a way to get him out of bed. She would play an incomplete chord on the piano. This so bothered her husband that he would get out of bed, go to the piano, and complete the chord. While he was up, his wife stripped the bed.[158]

• Two Quakers by the name of Rachel Kirk and Phillip Price got married. (Mr. Price was the 4th Superintendent of Westtown School.) Ms. Kirk was asked how she had ever consented to give up such a wonderful name as Kirk (which means "Church"). She replied, "Oh, I got a good Price for it."[159]

• Russian bass Feodor Chaliapine knew a military man named General Ernst, who sometimes quarreled with his wife. When the arguments grew especially heated, she would sit at the piano and play the Russian National Anthem, forcing the general to come to attention and stop quarreling.[160]

• When Morrie Turner, creator of the comic strip *Wee Pals*, wanted to propose to his girlfriend, Letha, he carefully prepared the words he wanted to speak to her, but he was so nervous when the time came to propose that all he could say at first was, "Will you, will you, will you?"[161]

• Many children's book illustrators put their spouses and children in their artistic creations. Jane Dyer once put her husband in an illustration in which she gave him striped socks and fairy wings. He requested that she not put him in any more illustrations.[162]

• French-American modern artist Marcel Duchamp enjoyed playing chess. In fact, on his honeymoon his wife got so annoyed at his chess playing that she glued all the chess pieces to the playing board. (They were divorced a few months later.)[163]

• Daniel Keyes wrote much of "Flowers for Algernon" on his typewriter at night while his wife, Aurea, was sleeping in the same room. She got so used to his typing that when he stopped she would wake up and ask, "What's the matter?"[164]

Illness

• Kazuko came from a very traditional Japanese family, but she ended up getting a Fulbright scholarship and moving to New York City. Once, she returned home when both of her parents were ill and in the hospital. Being a dutiful daughter, she spent time with both parents. Because they were on different floors, she would spend time with one parent, then go to a different floor and spend time with the other parent. This, however, was something that the lady who shared a room with her mother did not know. This lady's daughter was dutiful indeed, spending morning, afternoon, and evening with her. When Kazuko had to return to New York, this lady gave her a gift: a box of seaweed in a bag that had written on it traditional Japanese calligraphy. Kazuko thanked the lady for the gift, then carried it on board a train, where she fell asleep. When she woke up, she deciphered the calligraphy — and was horrified because it said, "Those who betray and do not take care of parents will be punished for not knowing the virtue of filial piety." While Kazuko had been sleeping, other Japanese people on the train had been able to read the calligraphy and receive the clear message that she was a bad daughter![165]

• When Quaker humorist Tom Mullen went into a hospital to have his colon removed, he met a nurse who had undergone the same medical procedure and so was able to answer his questions and joke with him about the procedure. For example, with no colon, the patient must wear a bag into which the feces collect. Mr. Mullen asked what he should do if the bag broke, and the nurse replied, "Stand downwind." The nurse also said that men have an advantage over women in undergoing this procedure: "Both men and women wear bags, but we women have to find shoes to match."[166]

Language

• Opera singer Helen Traubel was born in St. Louis, Missouri, at a time when the best opera singers were thought to come from Europe. In Seattle, a surprised woman told Ms. Traubel's husband, "Why, your wife speaks almost perfect English! How long has she been in this country?" Ms. Traubel's husband replied, "All her life, and if I told you how long that is, she would shoot me first and divorce me later."[167]

• As an elite figure skater, Sarah Hughes had the opportunity to compete in other countries while taking Spanish in high school. When she learned that she would compete in Mexico, she was excited about practicing her Spanish on the Mexicans. It didn't work out the way she expected, though, because the Mexicans were even more excited about practicing their English on Sarah.[168]

• Early in his career, Russian bass Feodor Chaliapine once knew an Italian ballerina named Tornaghi who danced in his country but was homesick for Italy. To comfort her, he used to say all the Italian words he knew at that time: *allegro andante religioso moderato*." (Later, he married her.)[169]

Letters

• Sid Fleischman, author of the McBroom comedy series of children's books, is a very good writer — so are many of the children who write him letters. In his autobiography, *The Abracadabra Kid*, Mr. Fleischman includes brief selections from some of the letters that children have written him. A few examples: "Dear Sid Fleischman, I have read *Mr. Mysterious & Company*. It is the second best book I ever read." "Dear Sid, I think for a man you write pretty good books." "Sorry I can't talk long, but I'm planning to write to the president."[170]

• Composer Franz Joseph Haydn married a woman who was difficult to get along with, and he was happy when his work took him away from her for long periods of time. During one occasion when Mr. Haydn was long away from his wife, a visitor asked him about several unopened letters piled up on his desk. Mr. Haydn replied, "They're from my wife. We write to each other every month, but I don't bother to open her letters, and I'm sure she doesn't open mine."[171]

• Amelia Earhart flew airplanes at a time when that was dangerous; therefore, at various times in her life, such as immediately before attempting to become the first woman passenger to fly across the

Atlantic Ocean, she wrote "popping-off" letters to her family and friends. These were letters that would be delivered to her family and friends if she died in the attempt to set a new record.[172]

• The *Wee Pals* comic strip features a rainbow of children of all races, both genders, and a few handicaps. Because of the black children in the comic strip, people sometimes wrote the strip's creator, Morrie Turner, to ask if he *really* knew any black people. He would write back, "Only my mother and father, my wife, and my son."[173]

• While working at Marvel Comics, Stan Lee wrote a "Soapbox" column. Of course, he received many, many letters asking many, many questions. One of his favorite letters asked him, "What do you want to be when you grow up?"[174]

Money

• As a Methodist preacher in Texas, Edwin Porter attended the Annual Conference every year. This was a big deal because at it he would find out to which church he would be assigned for the following year. A Porter family tradition was to take along one of the children to the Annual Conference when he or she reached the age of 11. Alyene Porter, the youngest daughter, wondered why this great privilege was given at the age of 11, instead of some other age. Brother Hugh speculated it was because at age 11 the children's understanding was more developed, but brother Paul Candler came up with a different reason: "It was the last year we could ride the train for half fare."[175]

• When telephone psychic Dougall Fraser was working for the Psychic Friends Network, a woman who called herself Champagne called him every morning at 11 a.m. to ask such questions as "When is my husband getting out of jail?" and "When am I getting my welfare check?" Finally, Mr. Fraser could stand it no longer and told her, "Champagne, the next time you want to call me, I want you to take $50, open a window, and throw it out. Because that's what you're doing every day. It is a complete waste of your money." She slammed down the telephone receiver and never called him again.[176]

• In 1978, running back Preston Pearson and his Dallas Cowboys lost in the Super Bowl to the Pittsburgh Steelers. As it happened, Mr. Pearson and his wife lived in Pittsburgh, and he gave his check for playing in the Super Bowl to his wife to deposit in a Pittsburgh bank. The bank teller looked at the size of the check, then told Mrs. Pearson that she was entitled to a free gift, although she might not want it. She didn't. The free gift was a recording of the Pittsburgh Steelers fight song.[177]

• Spanish painter Francisco Goya could be both generous and shrewd with his money. When his brother wanted to borrow money from him, Mr. Goya recognized that often relatives are very slow in repaying money borrowed from other family members. Therefore, Mr. Goya gave the money to a friend and told him to lend it to his brother without telling his brother the true source of the money.[178]

• When movie critic Roger Ebert was a child, he met J.C. Penney, the founder of the famous department store. Mr. Penney, then an old man, gave young Roger a penny and some financial advice — if you want dimes and dollars to take care of themselves, you need to take care of pennies and nickels. Roger saved ten cents, then he went to see a movie for nine cents. This left a penny, which he promptly invested in an all-day sucker.[179]

Mothers

• When Olympic gold medal-winning gymnast Kerri Strug was in the fourth grade, she spent six months working on a science project: a biosphere in a large aquarium. Unfortunately, when her brother drove her and her science project to school, he had to hit his brakes to avoid a collision with another car. The aquarium shattered, destroying six months of work, with dirt, water, frogs, and fish scattered everywhere. Fortunately, her mother was able to bring Kerri another aquarium, and they put the science project back together. However, Kerri told her mother, "This is the worst day of my life." Her mother then said something wise and wonderful: "I'll be happy if this is your worst day."

(For the worst day, it wasn't so bad — Kerri's science project won second prize.)[180]

• Soprano Beverly Sills stopped singing and taking voice lessons after giving birth to two children with handicaps. Muffy, her daughter, was a happy child, but she suffered from deafness. Peter, her son, suffered from mental retardation. Ms. Sills devoted much time to her children, but eventually her husband thought that it would be best if she did more than look after and help their children. Therefore, for her 33rd birthday, he gave her 52 round-trip airplane tickets between Boston, where they lived, and New York, where Estelle Liebling, her voice teacher, lived. Ms. Sills began taking voice lessons again, and she began singing in public again.[181]

• Children's book writer Phyllis Reynolds Naylor grew up during the Depression, when money was hard to come by. Entering kindergarten, she had only two dresses: one with red checks and one with blue checks. Her mother told her that if she alternated the dresses, wearing one the first day and the other the second day and so on, then everyone would think that she had more dresses than she really had. This made young Phyllis think how clever her mother was.[182]

• Nancy Stanford sat in a rocking chair to read a story to a group of first graders who sat at her feet. As she read the story, she felt a small hand rub her ankle, then her calf. Rather than disturb story time, she decided to continue reading the story to its end, then reprimand the child rubbing her leg. At the end of the story, she looked down, and a little boy told her, "Your leg feels just like my mother's." She did not reprimand the child.[183]

• Ezra Stone played the part of teenager Harry Aldrich on *The Aldrich Family* radio program. Following World War II, because space was lacking, he shared his dressing room with singer Jo Stafford. One day, his mother came to visit and was surprised to find his dressing room closet filled with frilly feminine garments. Mr. Stone, a happily married man, had to convince his mother that he was not keeping a mistress on the side.[184]

• Wilma Rudolph suffered from polio when she was a child, paralyzing her left leg. The doctors said that she would never walk again, but her mother told her that she would walk again. Ms. Rudolph says, "I believed my mother." After finally being able to walk without the aid of a brace, she starred on her high school basketball team. Later, she won gold in track at the 1960 Olympic Games.[185]

• Like her famous son, Mark Twain's mother was funny. As a boy, he was often ill. When his mother was 88 years old, he asked her about his early years, saying, "I suppose that during all that time you were uneasy about me?" She admitted that was true. Mr. Twain then asked her, "Afraid I wouldn't live?" His mother paused for a moment, then said, "No — afraid you would."[186]

• World-famous window dresser (and author) Simon Doonan and his sister loved their mother, Betty. Why? For one thing, upon request, she would take out her false teeth and recite the alphabet. Simon and his sister would be lying on the floor laughing hard even before she reached the unpronounceable (to people without teeth) letter H.[187]

• Once a mother, always a mother. Sculptor Louise Nevelson was justly proud of her son, Myron "Mike" Nevelson, who was also a sculptor. One of Mike's friends once heard him on the telephone talking to his mother. The middle-aged sculptor said, "Yes, Mother. Yes, I've eaten. I've *had* lunch. I *have* eaten, Mother."[188]

• Helen White Charles' mother, a Quaker, was often funny. One day, she was dining in a Germantown restaurant, and a waiter noticed that she hadn't finished her meal. The waiter asked, "You haven't eaten your steak. Why do you come in here?" She replied, "Oh, we like the waiters."[189]

• W.C. Fields, Jr., neither smoked nor drank, unlike his famous father. Why not? His mother had made him promise that he would not smoke or drink until he was 20 years old, and when he reached that age, he discovered that he did not want to smoke or drink.[190]

• The mother of *New Yorker* cartoonist George Booth gave him good advice: "Always stand upright. Act like you know what you're doing, even if you don't. Finally, no matter what you're getting paid, give it plenty of oomph!"[191]

• When Marc Cherry, the openly gay creator of TV's *Desperate Housewives*, came out to his mother, she told him, "Well, I'd love you even if you were a murderer." This line was so funny that he wrote it into the TV series.[192]

• A boy was showing off his new puppy. Asked whether it was a male or a female, he showed its belly side to his mother, who told him, "It's a boy." Her son told his friends, "She can tell just by looking at the bottoms of their feet."[193]

Music

• As a child, violinist Josef Gingold had a mother who was very supportive of his musical interests and of him. One Friday, a truant officer showed up at her house to tell her that Josef had missed school four Fridays in a row and was probably doing such things as playing pool with bums. Mrs. Gingold told the truant officer, "As a matter of fact, he's in the other room practicing." She then picked up a rolling pin and added, "He goes to the New York Philharmonic on Friday afternoons. Do me a favor, and leave this house. Next time I see your face, you're going to get it over the head."[194]

• When soprano Joan Hammond was a child, an accident severely scarred her left arm, so she always wore long-sleeved clothing when she grew up. At a concert in Australia, she wore long sleeves, upsetting a woman in the audience who said, "Why does she wear them? So ugly and old-fashioned! It spoils an evening's entertainment looking at them!" Unfortunately for the overly critical woman, Leo, Joan's brother, was in the audience, and he told her about Joan's childhood accident and resulting scars, then asked, "Do you come to a concert to criticize clothes or to listen to the music?"[195]

• Barbara Mandrell is a country singer with a long list of hits. She is also a Christian who sang to her young son Nathan three special songs: "Jesus Loves Me," "Jesus Loves the Little Children," and "This is the Day the Lord Has Made." She always wondered which of those songs young Nathan would sing first on his own, but the first song he actually sang on his own turned out to be, "All My Exes live in Texas."[196]

• When Walter Damrosch was a child, his father, Leopold, conducted Schubert's *Der häusliche Krieg*. Leopold thought it would be extravagant to hire a professional musician for a single cymbal crash, so he enlisted young Walter to do the honors. Unfortunately, at the performance, young Walter got stage fright, and when the time for the cymbal crash came, he froze and was unable to move his hands.[197]

Chapter 5: From Names to Work

Names

• Ohio University student Molly Gedeon had two names when she was growing up: Molly and Monica. When she was born, her parents tried to decide together on a name, but a mix-up occurred. Her mother thought that they had decided on the name Monica, but her father thought that they had decided on the name Molly. Therefore, although her birth certificate stated that her name was Monica, her father always called her Molly, which led to a little confusion at the schools she attended. When she was 18 years old, Monica legally had her name changed to Molly. That should solve the problem, right? Wrong! Her father immediately started calling her Monica! (The Gedeons are original. When Molly was a little girl, she was a member of a swim team, but she was one of the worst swimmers on the team. At one meet her family showed up wearing paper bags over their heads and carrying signs that said, "We're not with Gedeon!" Of course, when Molly saw them, she laughed so hard that she didn't hear when the race started and swam even more poorly than usual.)[198]

• When ballerina Chan Hon Goh was born, her mother was in a hospital and her father was performing as a dancer in a theater in Beijing. When he heard that his wife was giving birth, he rode his bicycle to the hospital, noticing as he rode a red full moon rising in the sky. He named her after the rising red moon — *Hon* means "red" and *Chan* means "To rise." When she was four years old, her mother taught her enough calligraphy to be able to write her nickname (*Da Hong* or "Big Red"), which she proceeded to do on the wall by the door of their apartment building. This horrified her parents because in communist China no one wanted to stand out in any way — it was much safer to blend in and be like everybody else. They covered up her nickname as quickly as they could.[199]

• The Right Reverend V. Gene Robinson has an unusual first name for a male. When he was born, he was paralyzed, and the attending physician thought that he would die within a few hours or days. The physician informed the parents, then said that he would need a name for the birth and the death certificates. V. Gene's parents had already picked out a name for a girl — Vicky Jean — and thinking that it wouldn't matter on a tombstone, they simply changed the name slightly to Vicky Gene. Of course, V. Gene got over his paralysis and grew up. Today, when he uses his credit card, he will often hear, "I'm sorry, sir. You can't use your wife's credit card."[200]

• Children's book author Tomie dePaola has an oddly spelled first name. At first, it was spelled the normal way, but little Tommy was a talented child who was sure to grow up to be famous, so a famous cousin of his mother — Irish tenor Morton Downey — gave him the new, unusual spelling. According to Mr. Downey, "He's got to have an unusual spelling for his first name so people will remember it." Everyone respected the new spelling for his name, except for his teachers at school, who made him spell it "Tommy," because that was the "correct" spelling.[201]

• Some people are more fanatical soccer fans than others. In 1982, Trevor George of Penarth, Wales, showed his love for the game by naming his infant daughter after 20 world-class soccer players. The baby's full name was Jennifer Edson Arentes do Nascimento Jairzinho Rivelino Carolos-Alberto Paulo Cesar Bretner Cruyff Greaves Charlton Best Moore Ball Keegan Banks Gray Francis Brooking Curtis Toshack Law George. His wife responded by promptly leaving home and having their daughter's name legally changed to Jennifer Anne George.[202]

• Joseph Epstein's father, Maurice, a successful businessman, donated money to charities, many of which gave him certificates and plaques and other forms of recognition. However, Joseph noticed on one plaque that his father's name was misspelled as "Moreese." This mistake did not bother his father, who replied, "For less than a $50,000 donation, you mustn't expect them to spell your name right."[203]

• When Penn Jillette (of Penn and Teller fame) and his wife, Emily, had their first child, they named her Moxie CrimeFighter Jillette. According to the proud father, "We chose her middle name because when she's pulled over for speeding she can say, 'But, officer, we're on the same side. My middle name is CrimeFighter.'" Penn's silent partner, Teller, had no official comment.[204]

• Edna St. Vincent Millay was often called "Vincent." The younger brother of her mother was a sailor who was seriously injured in a sea storm, then recovered his health in St. Vincent Hospital in New York City. To show her great gratitude, Edna's mother gave her the middle name of "St. Vincent."[205]

• When comedian Fred Allen was introduced to his future wife, Portland, he told her, "That is a ridiculous name." Unperturbed, she replied, "You should meet my sisters: Lebanon, Period, and Lastone."[206]

Politics

• Frances Hutt was the wife of Thomas Dewey, who ran for President against Harry S. Truman in 1948. The day of the election, it appeared that Mr. Dewey would win, so he asked his wife, "How do you like the idea of sleeping with the President of the United States?" She replied, "Of course it would be an honor, and one I can hardly wait to enjoy." However, once the votes were counted, Mr. Truman had been elected, so Ms. Hutt asked her husband, "Well, darling, will Harry be coming here or do I have to go to Washington?"[207]

• Feminist comedian Kate Clinton sometimes criticized President George W. Bush during her stand-up comedy. Of course, some people will get up and leave when she does that, so she likes to pretend that they have tiny bladders. As you would expect, she has been known to speak harshly of President Bush when she is among her friends. One day, as Ms. Clinton was talking about President Bush, her friend's three-year-old daughter gently touched her arm and said, "Please use your inside voice."[208]

• Shortly after getting married — and losing an election for a school committee — Calvin Coolidge ran into a man who said that he had voted for his opponent because anyone on the school board should have children in the public schools. Mr. Coolidge replied, "Might give me time."[209]

Practical Jokes

• Sarah Winchester was a very rich woman, as she inherited money made from sales of the gun that won the West. However, she worried about all the people who had been killed by Winchester rifles; in fact, she thought that the spirits of these people were haunting her. What to do? She consulted a medium who recommended that she provide a home for the spirits. In 1884, in San Jose, California, she bought an eight-room house for the spirits — but the house soon grew much bigger than eight rooms. The house eventually towered seven stories and contained 160 rooms — servants needed maps to find their way through the house. Interestingly, the spirits themselves designed the house. Each midnight, the spirits were consulted, and their wishes were followed. Apparently, spirits like chimneys, and so 47 were built. Also, apparently, spirits like practical jokes, so one door opened onto a blank wall, and another — not on the ground floor — opened onto thin air. One closet was only one inch deep, and a skylight was installed in a floor. After Sarah died, her heirs did not continue her design sessions with the spirits, but they did turn several of the rooms into the Winchester Rifle Museum.[210]

• Retired professor Sanford Pinsker helped play a notable practical joke on a science teacher. The teacher had set up an experiment to teach his students about electricity. In the experiment, the professor was supposed to throw a switch to complete an electrical circuit, which would result in the ringing of a bell. Unfortunately for the teacher, one of his students stationed himself by the electrical outlet and amused himself by unplugging the circuit. Of course, when the teacher threw the switch to complete the circuit and ring the bell, nothing happened. That's when Sanford said that the bell didn't ring because the teacher hadn't said "abracadabra." The teacher said, "That's ridiculous," but when Sanford said "abracadabra," then threw the switch, the bell rang. (The other student had plugged in the circuit again.) This happened a few more times, with the teacher throwing the switch and the bell not ringing, and with Sanford saying "abracadabra," throwing the switch, and ringing the bell. Finally, the teacher said, "abracadabra," then threw the switch — and the bell rang.[211]

• When he was a kid, Chicago Bear Walter Payton joined the Boy Scouts. On Walter's first camping trip, Scoutmaster Jim Walker told the kids a ghost story about a man who had been decapitated but who still put in an appearance whenever a bunch of kids were around making a lot of noise. (Hearing this, the kids grew quiet.) Later that night, after Mr. Walker had supposedly gone home, a figure in a sheet showed up. Panicking, the kids started shooting their .22s into the bushes. The figure — Mr. Walker, of course — started shouting, "Stop shooting!" Fortunately, they did, and Mr. Walker was not hurt. But later, as an adult, Mr. Payton felt bad when he thought about the headline that might have appeared in the newspapers: "BLACK SCOUT LEADER SLAIN BY SCOUTS. BODY FOUND COVERED WITH WHITE POWDER AND WRAPPED IN SHEET."[212]

• Young children tend to believe whatever you tell them. Quaker humorist Tom Mullen once showed his children the place where he had been born. The house had long been torn down, and at the location where the house had stood was an intersection with a flashing yellow light, so Mr. Mullen told his children that the flashing yellow light had been placed there in his honor. Afterward, whenever his children saw an intersection with a flashing yellow light, they asked, "Who was born there?"[213]

• In high school, author Beth Lisick had a truly original boyfriend. He could pass gas whenever he wanted, and for Christmas one year he gave her a toilet seat. Beth was quite original, too. After seeing a few too many catfights on the TV series *Dynasty*, Beth and her best friend, Amy, used to fake catfights in public places, rolling on the ground and pretending to kick each other and pull each other's hair until somebody stopped the "fight."[214]

Problem-Solving

• After Fanny Kemble married an American slave-owner in the days before the Civil War, she was shocked by the conditions that the slaves were forced to endure. The "infirmary" for sick slaves was filthy because the white men running the plantation wanted to be sure that it was more "pleasant" to work in the fields than to be in the infirmary. (Ms. Kemble used her own labor to clean up the infirmary and take care of the sick slaves.) In addition, because the mothers had to work in the fields, their infants were often entrusted to the care of very small children — some of these babysitters were almost babies themselves, being only four or five years old. As you would expect, the infants and small children were often very dirty. To keep the children clean, Ms. Kemble instituted a system of wages. To each owner of a clean face, she gave a penny. And if the infant the child was caring for also had a clean face, the child would get another penny. Very quickly, whenever she was surrounded by slave children, she was surrounded by slave children with clean faces.[215]

• May Pierstorff's parents were poor, but they were inventive. In 1914, when May was four years old, they decided to send her 100 miles away to visit her grandmother. Unfortunately, they could not afford the train fare. Therefore, they decided to mail her to her grandmother. They took May to the post office, and the postmaster looked at the regulations. Mail over 50 pounds could not be accepted; May weighed 48 pounds. No live animals could be sent through the mail — with the exception of baby chicks. The postmaster decided that May was a baby chick. He tagged the little girl's coat, and 53 cents in postage was affixed to the tag. She rode in the baggage car of the train under the watchful eye of the baggageman. When May reached her destination, a postal clerk delivered her to her grandmother.[216]

• Rabbi Meir was set upon by thieves in broad daylight, and when he returned home he decided to pray, using a passage from Psalms: "May sinners disappear from the earth and the wicked be no more." He prayed, but his wife, Beruriah, said that he was not praying properly. The words he was using were ambiguous: His words could be understood as asking for the deaths of the sinners. Instead, she said, he ought explicitly to pray for the other meaning of the words: Pray that the sinners reform and stop doing evil deeds, so that sinners and evil-doers would disappear from the earth by being transformed into godly people. Rabbi Meir agreed, saying, "As always, your wisdom astounds me. You are right. It is better to pray for a person to change than for a person to die." And he did as his wife advised.[217]

• Jonathan Eybeschuetz displayed remarkable intelligence even as a young child. One morning, a much bigger, anti-Semitic bully beat him up. While the beating was going on, he cried for the beating to stop so he could give the bully all the money he had. Of course, the bully stopped beating him, and young Jonathan emptied his pockets and handed over all his money to the bully. As he did so, he explained that today was a special Jewish holiday, and Jews were required to hand over all their money to anyone who beat them that day. Hearing this, the bully decided to beat up the richest Jew in town. Of course, the rich Jew cried out for help, and a police officer arrested the bully and took him to jail — exactly as young Jonathan had planned.[218]

• As a young child, young adult author Chris Crutcher had a terrible temper. It was so bad that he would jump into the air and then land on his back — hard. His mother was worried about this behavior, so she asked her family physician for advice. Dr. Patterson advised her to keep one of Chris' wooden blocks handy, and the next time he pulled that stunt, to roll the wooden block on the floor exactly where young Chris would land. The ploy worked. Landing on the wooden block was so painful that Chris did it exactly once.[219]

• After diving into shallow water, 16-year-old Joni Eareckson broke her neck and was paralyzed. Eventually, after months of being suspended in a Stryker frame, she recovered enough to be able to sit in a wheelchair. Dick, her boyfriend, sometimes visited her, but unfortunately, they ran into a problem: little privacy exists in a hospital. To solve the problem, they would go to an elevator and Dick would push the STOP button when they were in between floors. This gave them enough privacy to kiss.[220]

• A three-year-old boy fumbled while trying to button his coat, so his teacher, a Sister of Notre Dame, asked another, older boy, "Would you please help that little boy?" This was the wrong thing to say, and the little boy was deeply offended. He said, "I am a *big* boy." Thinking quickly, the Sister came up with exactly the right thing to say: "Will the bigger boy please help the big boy with his coat?" The little — uh, big — boy smiled.[221]

Proposals

• Apparently, the Orange Bowl Marathon in Miami, Florida, is a very romantic race to run. In 1980, Ken Gomberg and Debra Faillace were running together when Mr. Gomberg proposed to her at the 25-mile mark. In 1981, Bob Godwin and Ann Conlin were running together when Mr. Godwin proposed to her at the 18-mile mark. Both couples ended up crossing the finish line while holding hands.[222]

• The parents of choreographer Agnes George de Mille were Anna George and William de Mille. When Anna was 11 years old, and William was 12 years old, Anna asked him to marry her. He declined. But by the time Anna was 20 and William was 21, he had reconsidered his decision and proposed to her.[223]

• When Walter Prude proposed to Agnes de Mille, choreographer of *Oklahoma!* and *Rodeo: The Courting at Burnt Ranch*, she started crying. He asked, "In God's name, what's the matter? Surely this is not the first time someone's asked you?" Still crying, she replied, "No, but it's the first time I've said yes."[224]

Public Speaking

• Conductor Walter Damrosch became a radio celebrity when he hosted a program that brought classical music to youngsters. One day, he spoke at a children's school assembly. He was not introduced ahead of his address to the children, but as soon as he began speaking, the children recognized his voice and shouted, "It's Papa Damrosch! It's Papa Damrosch!"[225]

• Of course, President Lyndon B. Johnson was often introduced with many compliments and rhetorical flourishes. On occasions when the flattery was really poured on thick, he would say, "I wish my mother and father might have been here to hear that introduction. My father would have enjoyed it, and my mother would have believed it."[226]

Sex

• Emily Yoffe wrote the "Dear Prudence" advice column for the online magazine *Slate*. One of her columns that was more controversial than she had thought it would be gave advice to a young woman who was getting married and who wanted to remain childless. At the end of that column, Ms. Yoffe wrote that perhaps the young woman might want to rethink her decision to remain childless. In response to the criticisms that came pouring in, Ms. Yoffe pointed out that having a child around can be a source of very great pleasure even if it means missing out on such things as seeing new movies in the theater or having sex in the living room. For example, when her daughter was two years old and was being put to bed, she hugged Ms. Yoffe and said, "Mommy, you're a wonderful husband." According to Ms. Yoffe, "That was better than any of the movies I hadn't been to since she was born." (As for the sex, she and her husband do have sex — but not in the living room.)[227]

• Lefty Gomez was a great pitcher, but as happens to all pitchers who live long enough, his arm eventually went dead on him, and he began working for Wilson Sporting Goods. Once he was watching a Dodger workout, and after Carl Erskine had thrown batting practice, they began to compare notes on their families, with Lefty mentioning that his baby had just turned six months old. Sportswriter Jack Lang overheard this news, and he asked, "Lefty, did I hear you say you have a baby six months old at your age?" Lefty replied, "That was my *arm* that went dead."[228]

Siblings

• Edna St. Vincent Millay, often called by the name of Vincent, was the oldest of three daughters. While growing up, they helped their working mother by doing the housekeeping, which they made into a game, singing such songs as the Vincent-written "I'm the Queen of the Dishpans" while washing dishes. They also worked efficiently. For example, when they had to clean a room, Vincent would shout "Corner," then each sister would run to a corner and start cleaning as quickly as possible, working toward the middle of the room. Then all three sisters would work together to clean the fourth corner.[229]

• The large family of Frank B. Gilbreth, Jr., and Ernestine Gilbreth Carey lived in the early part of the 20th century. When the Gilbreth family liked someone and wanted him to become a relative through marriage, the young Gilbreths acted strangely. When Anne was being courted by a young doctor, her siblings found lots of reasons to leave her and Doctor Bob alone together and to turn out the lights of the room the young people were sitting in. Anne worried that her young beau might get the idea that her siblings had behaved that way with every boy she had ever known.[230]

• Many people think of the 1970s situation comedy *The Brady Bunch* as being very unrealistic and very different from the real world, but series creator Sherwood Schwartz points out that most of the episodes were based on things that happened in his family as he was growing up. In fact, he says that some of the episodes were "almost word for word" based on real life. Whenever someone tells Mr. Schwartz that families aren't like the Brady Bunch, he replies, "Maybe your family wasn't."[231]

Trailblazers

• Roberta Gibb (Bingay) was the first woman to successfully run and complete the Boston Marathon, but she had to run it in disguise — dressed as a man — because women were not allowed to run the Boston Marathon in 1966. Of course, some men running close to her discovered that she was a woman — and they supported her. Ms. Gibb remembers that they told her, "Gee, I wish my girlfriend would run." In 1983, she ran the Boston Marathon again — but this time she ran it legally as an honored trailblazer for women runners.[232]

• After aviator Amelia Earhart had set a record for women's long-distance flying, she received an effusive telegram: "Welcome, thrice welcome, Grand Lady of the Air, crowned glory of earth's womanhood!" The telegram amused Ms. Earhart, who gave it to her secretary and said, "Show this to G.P. [George Putnam, her husband], so he may appreciate me!"[233]

Valentine's Day

• Cameron Kelly wanted to use a novel way of proposing to his girlfriend, Angie Kreimer, so he wrote a 113-page marriage proposal, published it at <lulu.com>, using the title *50 Reasons Why You Should Marry Me ... And 51 Reasons Why I Should Marry You*, and gave her a copy as a Valentine's Day gift. In the proposal, she read reasons why she should marry him, including "I'm going to look like Sean Connery when I'm 65" and "You don't even have to change your initials." What was her one-word answer to the 113-page marriage proposal? It was Yes![234]

• French-cooking expert Julia Child and her husband seldom got their Christmas cards done in time to mail, so instead of Christmas cards they would send Valentine's Day cards to their friends. One card shows the happy couple taking a bubble bath together.[235]

War

• Elizabeth, the late Queen Mother, believed in sharing the pain and keeping a stiff upper lip when necessary. During World War II, she did not send her daughters — Elizabeth and Margaret — to the relative safety of the English countryside or to another country. Instead, she kept them in London even while the Nazis were dropping bombs frequently on the city and killing civilians. In addition, due to shortages the members of the royal family bathed in only four inches of water during the worst parts of the war. The Queen Mother even used tape on the bathtub to let her daughters know to what height they could fill the bathtub.[236]

• The grandfather of Meg Cabot, author of the best-selling *Princess Diaries* books, fought during World War II. He was a young soldier who was shot quickly after arriving in France. This sounds like bad news, but the result turned out to be good for him. Soon after he was shot, the other soldiers in his platoon raided the wine cellar of an abandoned farmhouse. Unfortunately, German soldiers had poisoned all of the bottles of wine, and so all the soldiers in the platoon died. According to Meg's grandfather, "Even being shot in the butt can have a silver lining." Meg's grandfather is the model for Princess Mia's grandfather on her father's side.[237]

Weddings

• Rabbi Aryeh Levine understood the feelings of other people. He once attended a wedding at which a hard-working but impoverished Jew of good character was asked to be a witness. The hard-working Jew gratefully agreed to be a witness, then a wealthy but proud Jew was asked to be a witness. The proud Jew was insulted at being asked to be a witness alongside another Jew of lesser wealth and status, so he declined the honor. This embarrassed the hard-working Jew. Rabbi Aryeh noticed that the hard-working Jew was embarrassed, so he immediately volunteered to be the other witness. Having such a renowned scholar as the second witness made both the hard-working Jew and the marrying couple very happy.[238]

• At a Jewish wedding, the groom smashes a glass with his foot. Why? It's a reminder that when the married couple argues — as all married couples do — they don't need to break each other's heart. Instead, they can break a glass. This is something that Rabbi Joseph H. Gelberman teaches each couple at weddings he performs. He once met a couple 10 years after he had married them, and he asked them how everything was. The husband replied, "Beautiful. We have three children, and everything is wonderful." Then he smiled and added, "But we have no glasses left."[239]

• Before modern dance pioneer Isadora Duncan went to Russia, she visited a fortune teller, who told her that she would get married — something that Ms. Duncan, who was philosophically opposed to marriage, scoffed at. However, she met a handsome Russian poet and soon was shocking her elderly language tutor by saying to her, "You'd better teach me what I ought to say to a beautiful man when I want to kiss him." And yes, she and the handsome poet were married.[240]

• Rabbi Morris N. Kertzer once officiated at a wedding of elderly people. The 76-year-old groom, whose best man was his grandson, was hard of hearing, and in the middle of the ceremony he thought the blessing was over so he gave his 69-year-old bride a passionate kiss. The grandson whispered to Rabbi Kertzer that to people as old as the groom and bride, time was precious.[241]

• At weddings of the *hasidim*, friends of the bridegroom used to steal the bridegroom's *tallit* (prayer shawl). To get it back, the bridegroom would have to pay a ransom of drinks for everybody. On one occasion, however, the bridegroom's *tallit* was given to a poor woman, and to get it back, the bridegroom, who could afford it, gave the poor woman a large sum of money.[242]

• Rabbi Morris N. Kertzer takes seriously his pre-marriage counseling of hopefully soon-to-be-wedded couples. One would-be groom, a medical student, thought little of his fiancé's plain looks, but spoke enthusiastically of how her family's money would help him establish a medical practice. Rabbi Kertzer would not marry him, suggesting instead that he find another rabbi to do the honors.[243]

• In 1925, Chicago Bears football player Duke Hanny wanted to skip a game so he could get married; unfortunately, his coach, George Halas, declined to let him skip the game. Big problem. Mr. Hanny showed up for the kickoff, started a fight with an opposing player just after the kickoff, was thrown out of the game, and went to his wedding. Problem solved.[244]

• Jascha Heifetz was a very popular violinist. When Josef Gingold (another excellent violinist) got married, the wedding guests disappeared quickly after the wedding ceremony. Why? That night, Heifetz was playing on the radio![245]

Work

• When Lindy Hop dancer Norma Miller was an infant, her recently widowed mother worried because she had two children to take care of. Her mother did not think that she could support herself and two children, so she went to an orphanage to have the people there take care of her children until she could take care of them. However, while she was at the orphanage, a little girl came up to her, tugged at her skirt, and asked, "Are you my mama?" Immediately, Norma's mother decided not to leave her children at the orphanage. Instead, she worked very hard for many hours at menial jobs to support herself and her children. As Norma grew up, her mother told her that she was working so hard at menial jobs because she wanted Norma to have long fingernails. That is why Ms. Miller always had — and has — long fingernails.[246]

• When she was in the fourth grade, writer Mary E. Lyons was taken on a field trip to a cotton field. She and the other children picked cotton for half an hour, then they were paid a dime. After paying the children, the owner of the cotton field invited the children to visit his country store. Because picking cotton was hard, hot, thirsty work, young Mary spent her dime on a bottle of Coca-Cola. When she grew up and remembered this experience, she realized that the owner of the cotton field and country store had probably paid a nickel for the bottle of Coca-Cola. He had gotten half an hour's work from young Mary and also made cash money.[247]

• Karen D. Beatty, RN, has this as her motto: "We'll get there!" For example, she is an African-American, and occasionally while working as a visiting nurse, she will sense that she is not welcome in some homes because of the color of her skin. Of course, if the patient requests a different nurse, she respects their wishes, but she will also tell herself, "We'll get there!" Even as a little girl, Ms. Beatty wanted to be a nurse because of one of her aunts who was a nurse. In first grade, she was given the assignment to make a paper doll. She made a paper nurse doll that had a brown face.[248]

• Halle Berry was born in Cleveland, Ohio, and she got her first name because her pregnant mother was shopping in Halle Brothers, a department store, and she decided that she liked the store's name. Before becoming a model and actress, Halle studied broadcast journalism at Cuyahoga Community College. She decided that this profession was not for her after she started crying while interviewing a family who had just lost their house in a fire.[249]

• Duffy and Sweeney (Jimmy Duffy and Fred Sweeney) were an early vaudeville comedy team. Once, they were fired, so Mr. Duffy and a small boy appeared at the office of the guy who had fired them. Mr. Duffy pointed to the boy and said, "Are you going to let him starve?" The comedy team was rehired, and the guy who had hired, fired, and rehired them never learned that the boy was not Mr. Duffy's son.[250]

Appendix A: Bibliography

Adler, Bill. *Baseball Wit*. New York: Crown Publishers Inc., 1986.

Atkinson, Margaret F. and May Hillman. *Dancers of the Ballet*. New York: Alfred A. Knopf, 1955.

Bauer, Marion Dane. *A Writer's Story: From Life to Fiction*. New York: Clarion Books, 1995.

Beckerman, Ilene. *Love, Loss, and What I Wore*. Chapel Hill, NC: Algonquin Books of Chapel Hill, 1995.

Benchley, Nathaniel. *Robert Benchley*. New York: McGraw-Hill Book Company, Inc., 1955.

Biracree, Tom. *Grandma Moses*. New York: Chelsea House Publishers, 1989.

Blum, David. *Quintet: Five Journeys Toward Musical Fulfillment*. Ithaca, NY, and London: Cornell University Press, 1999.

Blume, Judy, ed. *Places I Never Meant to Be: Original Stories by Censored Authors*. New York: Simon and Schuster Books for Young Readers, 1999.

Bourke, Dale Hanson. *Everyday Miracles: Holy Moments in a Mother's Day*. Dallas, TX: Word Publishing, 1989.

Bramhall, William. *The Great American Misfit*. New York: Clarkson N. Potter, Inc., 1982.

Brown, Michèle and Ann O'Connor. *Hammer and Tongues: A Dictionary of Women's Wit and Humour*. London: J.M. Dent and Sons, Ltd., 1986.

Cabot, Meg. *Holiday Princess*. New York: HarperCollins Publishers, Inc., 2005.

Cabot, Meg. *Perfect Princess*. New York: HarperCollins Publishers, Inc., 2004.

Cain, Michael. *Louise Nevelson*. New York: Chelsea House Publishers, 1989.

Certner, Simon, editor. *101 Jewish Stories for Schools, Clubs and Camps*. New York: Jewish Education Committee Press, 1961.

Chaliapine, Feodor Ivanovitch. *Pages From My Life: An Autobiography*. Trans. H.M. Buck. New York and London: Harper and Brothers, Publishers, 1927.

Charles, Helen White, collector and editor. *Quaker Chuckles and Other True Stories About Friends*. Oxford, OH: H.W. Charles, 1961.

Clinton, Kate. *What the L?* New York: Carroll & Graf Publishers, 2005.

Cohen, Sasha. *Fire on Ice: Autobiography of a Champion Figure Skater*. With Amanda Maciel. New York: HarperCollins Publishers, 2005.

Cossi, Olga. *Edna Hibel: Her Life and Art*. Lowell, MA: Discovery Enterprises, Ltd., 1994.

Crutcher, Chris. *King of the Mild Frontier*. New York: Greenwillow Books, 2003.

Cummings, Pat, compiler and editor. *Talking with Artists, Volume 3*. New York: Simon & Schuster Books for Young Readers, 1999.

Daffron, Carolyn. *Edna St. Vincent Millay*. New York: Chelsea House Publishers, 1989.

DeBartolo, Dick. *Good Days and MAD*. New York: Thunder's Mouth Press, 1994.

DeMott, Robert J. *Dave Smith: A Literary Archive*. Athens, OH: Ohio University Libraries, 2000.

dePaola, Tomie. *Here We All Are*. New York: G.P. Putnam's Sons, 2000.

dePaola, Tomie. *On My Way*. New York: G.P. Putnam's Sons, 2001.

Dole, Bob. *Great Presidential Wit*. New York: Scribner, 2001.

Doonan, Simon. *Wacky Chicks: Life Lessons from Fearlessly Inappropriate and Fabulously Eccentric Women*. New York: Simon & Schuster, 2003.

Donnelly, Liza. *Funny Ladies:* The New Yorker*'s Greatest Women Cartoonists and Their Cartoons*. Amherst, NY: Prometheus Books, 2005.

Duggleby, John. *Story Painter: The Life of Jacob Lawrence*. San Francisco, CA: Chronicle Books, 1998.

Epstein, Lawrence J. *Mixed Nuts: America's Love Affair with Comedy Teams From Burns and Allen to Belushi and Aykroyd*. New York: PublicAffairs, 2004.

Epstein, Lawrence J. *A Treasury of Jewish Inspirational Stories*. Northvale, NJ: Jason Aronson, Inc., 1993.

Ericsson, Mary Kentra. *Morrie Turner: Creator of "Wee Pals."* Chicago, IL: Childrens Press, 1986.

Erskine, Carl. *Carl Erskine's Tales from the Dodger Dugout*. Champaigne, IL: Sports Publishing Inc., 2000.

Evans, John D. *A Tom Sawyer Companion*. Lanham, MD: University Press of America, Inc., 1993.

Ewen, David. *Dictators of the Baton*. Chicago, IL: Ziff-Davis Publishing Company, 1948.

Feinberg, David B. *Queer and Loathing: Rants and Raves of a Raging AIDS Clone*. New York: Viking, 1994.

Fleischman, Sid. *The Abracadabra Kid*. New York: Greenwillow Books, 1996.

Freeman, Gillian, and Edward Thorpe. *Ballet Genius*. London: Equation, 1988.

Garner, Joe. *Stay Tuned: Television's Unforgettable Moments*. Kansas City, MO: Andrews McMeel Publishing, 2002.

Gaster, Moses. *The Exempla of the Rabbis: Being a Collection of Exempla, Apologues and Tales Culled from Hebrew Manuscripts and Rare Hebrew Books*. New York: Ktav Publishing House, Inc., 1968.

Gelberman, Rabbi Joseph H. *Zen Judaism: Teaching Tales of a Kabbalistic Rabbi*. With Lesley Sussman. Freedom, CA: The Crossing Press, 2001.

Gilbreth, Jr., Frank B. and Ernestine Gilbreth Carey. *Belles on Their Toes*. New York: Thomas Y. Crowell Company, 1950.

Glavich, Mary Kathleen, S.N.D. *Catholic School Kids Say the Funniest Things*. New York: Paulist Press, 2002.

Goh, Chan Hon. *Beyond the Dance: A Ballerina's Life*. With Cary Fagan. Toronto, Ontario, Canada: Tundra Books, 2002.

Goldin, Barbara Diamond. *A Child's Book of the Midrash: 52 Jewish Stories from the Sages*. Northvale, NJ: Jason Aronson Inc., 1990.

Govenar, Alan, collector and editor. *Stompin' at the Savoy: The Story of Norma Miller*. Cambridge, MA: Candlewick Press, 2006.

Green, Joey. *Hi Bob! The Unofficial Guide to* The Bob Newhart Show. New York: St. Martin's Griffin, 1996. Advance uncorrected proofs.

Greenberg, Jan, and Sandra Jordan. *Andy Warhol: Prince of Pop*. New York: Delacorte Press, 2004.

Greenberg, Jan, and Sandra Jordan. *Vincent van Gogh: Portrait of an Artist*. New York: Delacorte Press, 2001.

Hammond, Joan. *A Voice, A Life*. London: Victor Gollancz, Ltd., 1970.

Harmon, Jim. *The Great Radio Comedians*. Garden City, NY: Doubleday and Company, Inc., 1970.

Hasday, Judy L. *Agnes de Mille*. Philadelphia, PA: Chelsea House Publishers, 2004.

Henry, Linda Gambee, and James Douglas Henry. *The Soul of the Caring Nurse: Stories and Resources for Revitalizing Professional Passion*. Washington, D.C.: American Nurses Association, 2004.

Hill, L.A. *Elementary Anecdotes in American English*. New York: Oxford University Press, 1980.

Hoekstra, Molly, editor. *Am I Teaching Yet? Stories from the Teacher-Training Trenches*. Portsmouth, NH: Heinemann, 2002.

Hollingsworth, Amy. *The Simple Faith of Mister Rogers*. Nashville, TN: Integrity Publishers, 2005.

Jacobs, Linda. *Joan Moore Rice: The Olympic Dream*. St. Paul, MN: EMC Corporation, 1975.

Jacobsen, Peter. *Embedded Balls*. With Jack Sheehan. New York: G.P. Putnam's Sons, 2005.

Kertzer, Morris N. *Tell Me, Rabbi*. New York: Bloch Publishing Company, 1976.

Keyes, Daniel. *Algernon, Charlie and I: A Writer's Journey*. Boca Raton, FL: Challcrest Press Books, 1999.

Kindred, Dave. *Heroes, Fools, and Other Dreamers: A Sportswriter's Gallery of Extraordinary People*. Atlanta, GA: Longstreet Press, 1988.

Kinney, Jack. *Walt Disney and Other Assorted Characters: An Unauthorized Account of the Early Years at Disney's*. New York: Harmony Books, 1988.

Krull, Kathleen. *Lives of the Artists: Masterpieces, Messes (and What the Neighbors Thought)*. San Diego, CA: Harcourt Brace & Company, 1995.

Krull, Kathleen. *Lives of the Athletes: Thrills, Spills (And What the Neighbors Thought)*. San Diego, CA: Harcourt Brace and Company, 1997.

Laskas, Jeanne Marie. *We Remember: Women Born at the Turn of the Century Tell the Stories of Their Lives*. Photographs by Lynn Johnson. New York: William Morrow and Company, 1999.

Lawton, Mary. *Schumann-Heink: The Last of the Titans*. New York: The Macmillan Company, 1928.

Lee, Stan, and George Mair. *Excelsior! The Amazing Life of Stan Lee*. New York: Fireside, 2002.

Lewis, Gregg, and Deborah Shaw Lewis. *Today's Heroes: Joni Eareckson Tada*. Grand Rapids, MI: Zonderkidz, 2002.

Lipsyte, Robert. *Assignment: Sports*. New York: Harper & Row, Publishers, 1984.

Lisick, Beth. *Everybody into the Pool: True Tales*. New York: HarperCollins Publishers, Inc., 2005.

Little, Jean. *Little by Little: A Writer's Education*. Ontario, Canada: Viking Kestrel, 1987.

Lowry, Lois. *Looking Back: A Book of Memories*. Boston, MA: Houghton Mifflin Company, 1998.

Lyons, Mary E., editor. *Talking with Tebé: Clementine Hunter, Memory Artist*. Boston, MA: Houghton Mifflin Company, 1998.

Mason, Paul. *Sarah Michelle Gellar*. Chicago, IL: Raintree, 2005.

Meryman, Richard. *Andrew Wyeth*. New York: Harry N. Abrams, Inc., 1991.

Monteux, Fifi. *Everyone is Someone*. New York: Farrar, Straus and Cudahy, 1962.

Moore, Dudley. *Musical Bumps*. London: Robson Books, 1986.

Moore, H.S. *Liberty's Poet: Emma Lazarus*. Austin, TX: TurnKey Press, 2005.

Mullen, Tom. *Living Longer and Other Sobering Possibilities*. Richmond, IN: Friends United Press, 1996.

Nachman, Gerald. *Seriously Funny: The Rebel Comedians of the 1950s and 1960s*. New York: Pantheon Books, 2003.

Naylor, Phyllis Reynolds. *How I Came to Be a Writer*. New York: Aladdin Paperbacks, 1987.

Netzach, editor. *Chesed: The World is Built upon Kindness*. Edited and published by Netzach, a project of Mercaz HaTorah of California. North Hollywood, CA: Netzach, 1985.

Nixon, Joan Lowery. *The Making of a Writer*. New York: Delacorte Press, 2002.

O'Connell, Charles. *The Other Side of the Record*. New York: Alfred A. Knopf, 1949.

O'Connor, Barbara. *Barefoot Dancer: The Story of Isadora Duncan*. Minneapolis, MN: Carolrhoda Books, Inc., 1994.

Paolucci, Bridget. *Beverly Sills*. New York: Chelsea House Publishers, 1990.

Parsons, Larry A. *A Funny Thing Happened on the Way to the School Library*. Englewood, CO: Libraries Unlimited, Inc., 1990.

Porter, Alyene. *Papa was a Preacher*, New York: Abingdon Press, 1944.

Powers, Tom. *Steven Spielberg: Master Storyteller*. Minneapolis, MN: Lerner Publications Company, 1997.

Robbins, Trina. *Eternally Bad: Goddesses with Attitude*. Berkeley, CA: Conari Press, 2001.

Robbins, Trina. *The Great Women Cartoonists*. New York: Watson-Guptill Publications, 2001.

Rockwell, Bart. *World's Strangest Baseball Stories*. Mahwah, N.J.: Watermill Press, 1993.

Rockwell, Bart. *World's Strangest Football Stories*. Mahwah, N.J.: Watermill Press, 1993.

Rogers, Fred. *The World According to Mister Rogers*. New York: Hyperion, 2003.

Rolph, Daniel N. *My Brother's Keeper: Union and Confederate Soldiers' Acts of Mercy during the Civil War*. Mechanicsburg, PA: Stackpole Books, 2002.

Rooney, Frances, editor. *Hear Me Out: True Stories of Teens Educating and Confronting Homophobia*. Toronto, Ontario, Canada: Second Story Press, 2004. A project of Planned Parenthood of Toronto.

Rubin, Susan Goldman. *Frank Lloyd Wright*. New York: Harry N. Abrams, Inc., 1994.

Samra, Cal and Rose, editors. *Holy Hilarity*. Colorado Springs, CO: WaterBrook Press, 1999.

Samra, Cal and Rose, editors. *More Holy Humor*. Colorado Springs, CO: WaterBrook Press, 1997.

Schuman, Michael A. *Halle Berry: "Beauty is Not Merely Physical."* Berkeley Heights, NJ: Enslow Publishers, Inc., 2006.

Schuman, Michael A. *Will Smith: "I Like Blending a Message with Comedy."* Berkeley Heights, NJ: Enslow Publishers, Inc., 2006.

Schwager, Tina, and Michele Schuerger. *Gutsy Girls: Young Women Who Dare.* New York: Scholastic, Inc., 1999.

Scott, John Anthony. *Fanny Kemble's America.* New York: Thomas Y. Crowell Company, 1973.

Seidman, David. *Jerry Spinelli.* New York: The Rosen Publishing Group, Inc., 2004.

Shore, Nancy. *Amelia Earhart.* New York: Chelsea House Publishers, 1987.

Sivorinovsky, Alina. *Sarah Hughes: Skating to the Stars.* New York: Berkley Books, 2001.

Sleator, William. *Oddballs.* New York: Dutton's Children's Books, 1993.

Sobol, Donald J. *Encyclopedia Brown's Book of Wacky Sports.* New York: William Morrow and Company, 1984.

Sommers, Michael A. *Chris Crutcher.* New York: The Rosen Publishing Group, 2005.

Speaker-Yuan, Margaret. *Agnes de Mille.* New York: Chelsea House Publishers, 1990.

Strug, Kerri. *Heart of Gold.* With Greg Brown. Dallas, TX: Taylor Publishing Company, 1996.

Strug, Kerri. *Landing on My Feet: A Diary of Dreams.* With John P. Lopez. Kansas City, MO: Andrews McMeel Publishing, 1997.

Sufrin, Mark. *Payton.* New York: Charles Scribner's Sons, 1988.

Traubel, Helen. *St. Louis Woman.* New York: Duell, Sloan and Pearce, 1959.

True, Cynthia. *American Scream: The Bill Hicks Story.* New York: HarperEntertainment, 2002.

Uchida, Yoshiko. *The Invisible Thread.* New York: Beech Tree Books, 1991.

Van Dyke, Dick. *Faith, Hope and Hilarity.* Edited by Ray Parker. Garden City, NY: Doubleday and Company, Inc, 1970.

Van Dyke, Dick. *Those Funny Kids!* Garden City, NY: Doubleday and Company, Inc., 1975.

Waldron, Ann. *Francisco Goya.* New York: Harry N. Abrams, Inc., 1992.

Wulffson, Don L. *Amazing True Stories.* New York: Cobblehill Books, 1991.

Zymet, Cathy Alter. *Backstreet Boys.* Philadelphia, PA: Chelsea House Publishers, 2001.

Appendix B: About the Author

It was a dark and stormy night. Suddenly a cry rang out, and on a hot summer night in 1954, Josephine, wife of Carl Bruce, gave birth to a boy — me. Unfortunately, this young married couple allowed Reuben Saturday, Josephine's brother, to name their first-born. Reuben, aka "The Joker," decided that Bruce was a nice name, so he decided to name me Bruce Bruce. I have gone by my middle name — David — ever since.

Being named Bruce David Bruce hasn't been all bad. Bank tellers remember me very quickly, so I don't often have to show an ID. It can be fun in charades, also. When I was a counselor as a teenager at Camp Echoing Hills in Warsaw, Ohio, a fellow counselor gave the signs for "sounds like" and "two words," then she pointed to a bruise on her leg twice. Bruise Bruise? Oh yeah, Bruce Bruce is the answer!

Uncle Reuben, by the way, is the guy who gave me a haircut when I was in kindergarten. He cut my hair short and shaved a small bald spot on the back of my head. My mother wouldn't let me go to school until the bald spot grew out again.

Of all my brothers and sisters (six in all), I am the only transplant to Athens, Ohio. I was born in Newark, Ohio, and have lived all around Southeastern Ohio. However, I moved to Athens to go to Ohio University and have never left.

At Ohio U, I never could make up my mind whether to major in English or Philosophy, so I got a bachelor's degree with a double major in both areas, then I added a Master of Arts degree in English and a Master of Arts degree in Philosophy. Yes, I have my MAMA degree.

Currently, and for a long time to come (I eat fruits and veggies), I am spending my retirement writing books such as *Nadia Comaneci: Perfect 10*, *The Funniest People in Comedy*, *Homer's* Iliad: *A Retelling in Prose*, and *William Shakespeare's* Hamlet: *A Retelling in Prose*.

If all goes well, I will publish one or two books a year for the rest of my life. (On the other hand, a good way to make God laugh is to tell Her your plans.)

By the way, my sister Brenda Kennedy writes romances such as *A New Beginning* and *Shattered Dreams*.

Appendix C: Some Books by David Bruce

Anecdote Collections

250 Anecdotes About Opera
250 Anecdotes About Religion
250 Anecdotes About Religion: Volume 2
250 Music Anecdotes
Be a Work of Art: 250 Anecdotes and Stories
The Coolest People in Art: 250 Anecdotes
The Coolest People in the Arts: 250 Anecdotes
The Coolest People in Books: 250 Anecdotes
The Coolest People in Comedy: 250 Anecdotes
Create, Then Take a Break: 250 Anecdotes
Don't Fear the Reaper: 250 Anecdotes
The Funniest People in Art: 250 Anecdotes
The Funniest People in Books: 250 Anecdotes
The Funniest People in Books, Volume 2: 250 Anecdotes
The Funniest People in Books, Volume 3: 250 Anecdotes
The Funniest People in Comedy: 250 Anecdotes
The Funniest People in Dance: 250 Anecdotes
The Funniest People in Families: 250 Anecdotes
The Funniest People in Families, Volume 2: 250 Anecdotes
The Funniest People in Families, Volume 3: 250 Anecdotes
The Funniest People in Families, Volume 4: 250 Anecdotes
The Funniest People in Families, Volume 5: 250 Anecdotes
The Funniest People in Families, Volume 6: 250 Anecdotes
The Funniest People in Movies: 250 Anecdotes
The Funniest People in Music: 250 Anecdotes
The Funniest People in Music, Volume 2: 250 Anecdotes
The Funniest People in Music, Volume 3: 250 Anecdotes
The Funniest People in Neighborhoods: 250 Anecdotes
The Funniest People in Relationships: 250 Anecdotes
The Funniest People in Sports: 250 Anecdotes
The Funniest People in Sports, Volume 2: 250 Anecdotes
The Funniest People in Television and Radio: 250 Anecdotes
The Funniest People in Theater: 250 Anecdotes

The Funniest People Who Live Life: 250 Anecdotes
The Funniest People Who Live Life, Volume 2: 250 Anecdotes
The Kindest People Who Do Good Deeds, Volume 1: 250 Anecdotes
The Kindest People Who Do Good Deeds, Volume 2: 250 Anecdotes
Maximum Cool: 250 Anecdotes
The Most Interesting People in Movies: 250 Anecdotes
The Most Interesting People in Politics and History: 250 Anecdotes
The Most Interesting People in Politics and History, Volume 2: 250 Anecdotes
The Most Interesting People in Politics and History, Volume 3: 250 Anecdotes
The Most Interesting People in Religion: 250 Anecdotes
The Most Interesting People in Sports: 250 Anecdotes
The Most Interesting People Who Live Life: 250 Anecdotes
The Most Interesting People Who Live Life, Volume 2: 250 Anecdotes
Reality is Fabulous: 250 Anecdotes and Stories
Resist Psychic Death: 250 Anecdotes
Seize the Day: 250 Anecdotes and Stories

[1] Source: Margaret Speaker-Yuan, *Agnes de Mille*, p. 81.

[2] Source: Fred Rogers, *The World According to Mister Rogers*, p. 3.

[3] Source: Fifi Monteux, *Everyone is Someone*, pp. 51-54.

[4] Source: Marion Dane Bauer, *A Writer's Story*, pp. 75-76.

[5] Source: Lois Lowry, *Looking Back: A Book of Memories*, pp. 63-64.

[6] Source: Susan Goldman Rubin, *Frank Lloyd Wright*, p. 84.

[7] Source: Don L. Wulffson, *Amazing True Stories*, pp. 32-33.

[8] Source: Dick Van Dyke, *Faith, Hope, and Hilarity*, p. 47.

[9] Source: Robert Lipsyte, *Assignment: Sports*, p. 130.

[10] Source: Joan Hammond, *A Voice, A Life*, pp. 163-164.

[11] Source: Jan Greenberg and Sandra Jordan, *Vincent van Gogh: Portrait of an Artist*, pp. 105-106.

[12] Source: Michael Cain, *Louise Nevelson*, p. 77.

[13] Source: Jan Greenberg and Sandra Jordan, *Vincent van Gogh: Portrait of an Artist*, p. 45.

[14] Source: Jan Greenberg and Sandra Jordan, *Andy Warhol: Prince of Pop*, pp. 30-31.

[15] Source: Tomie dePaola, *Here We All Are*, pp. 66- 68.

[16] Source: Amy Hollingsworth, *The Simple Faith of Mister Rogers*, p. 155.

[17] Source: Bill Adler, *Baseball Wit*, p. 105.

[18] Source: Trina Robbins, *The Great Women Cartoonists*, p. 85.

[19] Source: Bart Rockwell, *World's Strangest Baseball Stories*, p. 54.

[20] Source: Cal and Rose Samra, *Holy Hilarity*, pp. 129-130.

[21] Source: Yoshiko Uchida, *The Invisible Thread*, pp. 44-45.

[22] Source: Joan Lowery Nixon, *The Making of a Writer*, pp. 31-33.

[23] Source: Jean Little, *Little by Little: A Writer's Education*, pp. 222-223.

[24] Source: Moses Gaster, *The Exempla of the Rabbis*, pp. 169-179.

[25] Source: Daniel Keyes, *Algernon, Charlie and I: A Writer's Journey*, pp. 61-62, 64-66.

[26] Source: Alina Sivorinovsky, *Sarah Hughes: Skating to the Stars*, pp. 10, 12-15.

[27] Source: Tomie dePaola, *On My Way*, pp. 60-65.

[28] Source: Judy Blume, ed., *Places I Never Meant to Be: Original Stories by Censored Authors*, pp. 1-2.

[29] Source: Simon Certner, editor, *101 Jewish Stories for Schools, Clubs and Camps*, p. 176.

[30] Source: Beth Lisick, *Everybody into the Pool*, pp. 17, 137-138.

[31] Source: Susan Goldman Rubin, *Frank Lloyd Wright*, pp. 38, 40, 48-49.

[32] Source: Lois Lowry, *Looking Back: A Book of Memories*, p. 51.

[33] Source: Dale Hanson Bourke, *Everyday Miracles*, pp. 61-63.

[34] Source: Yoshiko Uchida, *The Invisible Thread*, pp. 11-12.

[35] Source: Carl Erskine, *Carl Erskine's Tales from the Dodger Dugout*, p. 38.

[36] Source: David Seidman, *Jerry Spinelli*, pp. 7-8.

[37] Source: Fifi Monteux, *Everyone is Someone*, pp. 69-70.

[38] Source: Olga Cossi, *Edna Hibel: Her Life and Art*, p. 42.

[39] Source: Linda Jacobs, *Joan Moore Rice: The Olympic Dream*, p. 14.

[40] Source: Richard Meryman, *Andrew Wyeth*, p. 42.

[41] Source: Sasha Cohen, *Fire on Ice*, pp. 4-5.

[42] Source: Larry A. Parsons, *A Funny Thing Happened on the Way to the School Library*, p. 7.

[43] Source: Paul Mason, *Sarah Michelle Gellar*, p. 7.

[44] Source: Amy Hollingsworth, *The Simple Faith of Mister Rogers*, pp. 64-65.

[45] Source: Margaret F. Atkinson and May Hillman, *Dancers of the Ballet*, p. 23.

[46] Source: Mark Sufrin, *Payton*, p. 29.

[47] Source: Jean Little, *Little by Little: A Writer's Education*, p. 50.

[48] Source: Ilene Beckerman, *Love, Loss, and What I Wore*, p. 10.

[49] Source: Michèle Brown and Ann O'Connor, *Hammer and Tongues*, p. 151.

[50] Source: Tom Powers, *Steven Spielberg: Master Storyteller*, p. 80.

[51] Source: Kerri Strug, *Heart of Gold*. This book has unnumbered pages.

[52] Source: Cathy Alter Zymet, *Backstreet Boys*, pp. 20-21.

[53] Source: Jan Greenberg and Sandra Jordan, *Andy Warhol: Prince of Pop*, pp. 2-3.

[54] Source: John D. Evans, *A Tom Sawyer Companion*, p. 37.

[55] Source: Julie Reid, "'I'd like to have seen you,' my mother says, 'but it's not as important as people think.'" 1 August 2006 <http://www.guardian.co.uk/g2/story/0,,1834502,00.html>.

[56] Source: Mary Lawton, *Schumann-Heink: The Last of the Titans*, p. 162.

[57] Source: Cal and Rose Samra, editors, *More Holy Humor*, p. 48.

[58] Source: Marion Dane Bauer, *A Writer's Story*, pp. 23-25.

[59] Source: Michael A. Sommers, *Chris Crutcher*, p. 24.

[60] Source: Mary Lawton, *Schumann-Heink: The Last of the Titans*, pp. 302, 304.

[61] Source: Kathleen Krull, *Lives of the Athletes*, p. 76.

[62] Source: Bette Howland, "The Escape Artist." 13 May 2006 <http://www.commentarymagazine.com/article.asp?aid=12105054_1>.

[63] Source: Nathaniel Benchley, *Robert Benchley*, p. 192.

[64] Source: Cynthia True, *American Scream: The Bill Hicks Story*, pp. 261-262.

[65] Source: Meg Cabot, *Holiday Princess*, p. 66.

[66] Source: Ilene Beckerman, *Love, Loss, and What I Wore*, p. 58.

[67] Source: H.S. Moore, *Liberty's Poet: Emma Lazarus*, pp. 60-61.

[68] Source: Gerald Nachman, *Seriously Funny*, pp. 219-221.

[69] Source: Lawrence J. Epstein, *Mixed Nuts*, p. 170.

[70] Source: Gerald Nachman, *Seriously Funny*, p. 335.

[71] Source: Alyene Porter, *Papa was a Preacher*, p. 156.

[72] Source: Paul Mason, *Sarah Michelle Gellar*, p. 35.

[73] Source: Meg Cabot, *Perfect Princess*, pp. 71-72.

[74] Source: Liza Donnelly, *Funny Ladies*, p. 37.

[75] Source: Chan Hon Goh, *Beyond the Dance: A Ballerina's Life*, pp. 48-49.

[76] Source: Judy L. Hasday, *Agnes de Mille*, pp. 24-25.

[77] Source: Margaret F. Atkinson and May Hillman, *Dancers of the Ballet*, p. 8.

[78] Source: Lucy Mangan, "To you, my darling, I leave very little ...." 28 July 2006 <http://www.guardian.co.uk/g2/story/0,,1832032,00.html>.

[79] Source: Cal and Rose Samra, *Holy Hilarity*, pp. 85-86.

[80] Source: Tom Biracree, *Grandma Moses*, p. 42, 52.

[81] Source: David B. Feinberg, *Queer and Loathing: Rants and Raves of a Raging AIDS Clone*, p. 89.

[82] Source: L.A. Hill, *Elementary Anecdotes in American English*, p. 10.

[83] Source: Joe Garner, *Stay Tuned: Television's Unforgettable Moments*, p. 52.

[84] Source: Chris Crutcher, *King of the Mild Frontier*, pp. 97-105.

[85] Source: Tomie dePaola, *On My Way*, pp. 68-75.

[86] Source: John Duggleby, *Story Painter: The Life of Jacob Lawrence*, p. 22.

[87]Source: Barbara Diamond Goldin, *A Child's Book of the Midrash: 52 Jewish Stories from the Sages*, p. 38.

[88] Source: Freeman J. Dyson, "Wise Man." 20 October 2005 <http://www.nybooks.com/articles/18350>.

[89] Source: Rabbi Joseph H. Gelberman, *Zen Judaism: Teaching Tales of a Kabbalistic Rabbi*, pp. 104-5. The pages of this volume are unnumbered, but I started counting with the Introduction as page 1.

[90] Source: Mary Kathleen Glavich, S.N.D., *Catholic School Kids Say the Funniest Things*, p. 85.

[91] Source: Dave Kindred, *Heroes, Fools, and Other Dreamers*, p. 8.

[92] Source: Arlene Istar Lev, "Gay parents and gender-bending children." 11 July 2006 <http://www.advocate.com/exclusive_detail_ektid33585.asp>.

[93] Source: William Sleator, *Oddballs*, p. 115.

[94] Source: Chris Crutcher, *King of the Mild Frontier*, p. 84.

[95] Source: Simon Certner, editor, *101 Jewish Stories for Schools, Clubs and Camps*, p. 6.

[96] Source: Anna Quindlen, 'Be Not Afraid,' a commencement address delivered May 17, 2005 to Barnard College. <http://www.beliefnet.com/story/167/story_16749_1.html>.

[97] Source: Anna Quindlen, 'Be Not Afraid,' a commencement address delivered May 17, 2005 to Barnard College. <http://www.beliefnet.com/story/167/story_16749_1.html>.

[98] Source: Stuart Jeffries, "'I'm a celebrity, get me an honorary degree!'" 6 July 2006 <http://www.guardian.co.uk/g2/story/0,,1813415,00.html>.

[99] Source: Robert J. DeMott, *Dave Smith: A Literary Archive*, p. xiii.

[100] Source: Judy Blume, ed., *Places I Never Meant to Be: Original Stories by Censored Authors*, p. 161.

[101] Source: Michael A. Schuman, *Will Smith: "I Like Blending a Message with Comedy,"* pp. 17, 19.

[102] Source: Molly Hoekstra, editor, *Am I Teaching Yet?*, pp. 111-112.

[103] Source: Dave Kindred, *Heroes, Fools, and Other Dreamers*, p. 45.

[104] Source: L.A. Hill, *Elementary Anecdotes in American English*, p. 8.

[105] Source: Molly Hoekstra, editor, *Am I Teaching Yet?*, p. 26.

[106] Source: Cynthia True, *American Scream: The Bill Hicks Story*, p. 3.

[107] Source: Gillian Freeman and Edward Thorpe, *Ballet Genius*, p. 30.

[108] Source: Michael A. Schuman, *Will Smith: "I Like Blending a Message with Comedy,"* pp. 14-15.

[109] Source: Joan Lowery Nixon, *The Making of a Writer*, pp. 20-23.

[110] Source: Frank B. Gilbreth, Jr. and Ernestine Gilbreth Carey, *Cheaper by the Dozen*, p. 3.

[111] Source: Kerri Strug, *Landing on My Feet*, pp. 120-121.

[112] Source: Joey Green, *Hi Bob!*, p. 10.

[113] Source: Kate Clinton, *What the L?*, pp. 228-230.

[114] Source: Andrew Tobias, "What's Wrong with This Picture?" 13 May 2005 <http://www.andrewtobias.com/newcolumns/050513.html>.

[115] Source: Peter Jacobsen, *Embedded Balls*, p. 51.

[116] Source: Tina Schwager and Michele Schuerger, *Gutsy Girls*, pp. 17-18.

[117] Source: Frances Rooney, editor, *Hear Me Out: True Stories of Teens Educating and Confronting Homophobia*, p. 164.

[118] Source: Kerri Strug, *Landing on My Feet*, p. 6.

[119] Source: Bill Adler, *Baseball Wit*, p. 31.

[120] Source: Dick DeBartolo, *Good Days and MAD*, pp. 244-245, 249.

[121] Source: Sasha Cohen, *Fire on Ice*, pp. 8, 10-11.

[122] Source: Trina Robbins, *Eternally Bad: Goddesses with Attitude*, pp. 43-44.

[123] Source: David B. Feinberg, *Queer and Loathing: Rants and Raves of a Raging AIDS Clone*, pp. 208-209.

[124] Source: Charles O'Connell, *The Other Side of the Record*, pp. 100-101.

[125] Source: Nathaniel Benchley, *Robert Benchley*, p. 212.

[126] Source: Dick Van Dyke, *Faith, Hope, and Hilarity*, p. 136.

[127] Source: William Sleator, *Oddballs*, pp. 118-119.

[128] Source: Stan Lee and George Mair, *Excelsior! The Amazing Life of Stan Lee*, pp. 14-15.

[129] Source: Bridget Paolucci, *Beverly Sills*, p. 27.

[130] Source: Sid Fleischman, *The Abracadabra Kid*, p. 154.

[131] Source: Dick Van Dyke, *Those Funny Kids!*, p. 14.

[132] Source: Tina Schwager and Michele Schuerger, *Gutsy Girls*, pp. 43, 45-46. Also: "Diver happy to play a role in whale rescue." Good News Blog. 31 July 2005 <http://www.goodnewsblog.com/2005/07/31/diver-happy-to-play-a-role-in-whale-rescue>. Also: "Tangled GB whale gets helping hand. South Africa." Tursipos.org. 4 August 2005 <http://tursiops.org/modules.php?name=News&file=print&sid=1480>.

[133] Source: Daniel N. Rolph, *My Brother's Keeper*, p. 82.

[134] Source: Daniel N. Rolph, *My Brother's Keeper*, pp. 79-80.

[135] Source: Phyllis Reynolds Naylor, *How I Came to Be a Writer*, pp. 129-130.

[136] Source: Dale Hanson Bourke, *Everyday Miracles*, pp. 96-97.

[137] Source: Tom Biracree, *Grandma Moses*, pp. 64, 73.

[138] Source: Fred Rogers, *The World According to Mister Rogers*, p. 24.

[139] Source: Olga Cossi, *Edna Hibel: Her Life and Art*, p. 120.

[140] Source: Linda Gambee Henry and James Douglas Henry, *The Soul of the Caring Nurse*, pp. 8-9.

[141] Source: Barbara O'Connor, *Barefoot Dancer: The Story of Isadora Duncan*, pp. 67-68.

[142] Source: Trina Robbins, *Eternally Bad: Goddesses with Attitude*, p. 36.

[143] Source: Dick DeBartolo, *Good Days and MAD*, pp. 60-61.

[144] Source: Richard Meryman, *Andrew Wyeth*, pp. 71, 74.

[145] Source: Linda Jacobs, *Joan Moore Rice: The Olympic Dream*, pp. 7-8, 11, 32.

[146] Source: Joey Green, *Hi Bob!*, p. 11.

[147] Source: Trina Robbins, *The Great Women Cartoonists*, pp. 2, 5, 8.

[148] Source: Jack Kinney, *Walt Disney and Other Assorted Characters*, p. 160.

[149] Source: Moses Gaster, *The Exempla of the Rabbis*, pp. 55-56.

[150] Source: Helen Traubel, *St. Louis Woman*, pp. 75.

[151] Source: Netzach, editor, *Chesed: The World is Built upon Kindness*, p. 27.

[152] Source: David Seidman, *Jerry Spinelli*, pp. 25-26.

[153] Source: Jeanne Marie Laskas, *We Remember*, pp. 35-37.

[154] Source: Roger Ebert, "Here's to Anne Bancroft (1931-2005)." 8 June 2005 <http://rogerebert.suntimes.com/apps/pbcs.dll/article?AID=/20050607/PEOPLE/506080301>.

[155] Source: Jeanne Marie Laskas, *We Remember*, p. 40.

[156] Source: Kathleen Krull, *Lives of the Artists*, p. 22.

[157] Source: Tom Powers, *Steven Spielberg: Master Storyteller*, p. 111.

[158] Source: Dudley Moore, *Musical Bumps*, p. 52.

[159] Source: Helen White Charles, collector and editor, *Quaker Chuckles*, p. 80.

[160] Source: Feodor Ivanovitch Chaliapine, *Pages From My Life: An Autobiography*, p. 142.

[161] Source: Mary Kentra Ericsson, *Morrie Turner: Creator of "Wee Pals,"* p. 58.

[162] Source: Pat Cummings, compiler and editor, *Talking with Artists, Volume 3*, p. 33.

[163] Source: Kathleen Krull, *Lives of the Artists*, p. 67.

[164] Source: Daniel Keyes, *Algernon, Charlie and I: A Writer's Journey*, p. 97.

[165] Source: Simon Doonan, *Wacky Chicks*, p. 205.

[166] Source: Tom Mullen, *Living Longer and Other Sobering Possibilities*, p. 9.

[167] Source: Helen Traubel, *St. Louis Woman*, pp. 243-244.

[168] Source: Alina Sivorinovsky, *Sarah Hughes: Skating to the Stars*, pp. 51-52.

[169] Source: Feodor Ivanovitch Chaliapine, *Pages From My Life: An Autobiography*, p. 179.

[170] Source: Sid Fleischman, *The Abracadabra Kid*, pp. 1, 5, 9.

[171] Source: Dudley Moore, *Musical Bumps*, pp. 45-46.

[172] Source: Nancy Shore, *Amelia Earhart*, p. 50.

[173] Source: Mary Kentra Ericsson, *Morrie Turner: Creator of "Wee Pals,"* p. 69.

[174] Source: Stan Lee and George Mair, *Excelsior! The Amazing Life of Stan Lee*, p. 151.

[175] Source: Alyene Porter, *Papa was a Preacher*, pp. 73-74.

[176] Source: Dougall Fraser, "Bells Are Ringing!" May 2005 <http://www.beliefnet.com/story/166/story_16671_1.html>.

[177] Source: Bart Rockwell, *World's Strangest Football Stories*, p. 53.

[178] Source: Ann Waldron, *Francisco Goya*, p. 27.

[179] Source: Roger Ebert, "Plowing Field's won't grow business." 22 September 2005 <http://rogerebert.suntimes.com/apps/pbcs.dll/article?AID=/20050922/COMMENTARY/509220301>.

[180] Source: Kerri Strug, *Heart of Gold*. This book has unnumbered pages.

[181] Source: Bridget Paolucci, *Beverly Sells*, pp. 50-53.

[182] Source: Phyllis Reynolds Naylor, *How I Came to Be a Writer*, pp. 2-3.

[183] Source: Larry A. Parsons, *A Funny Thing Happened on the Way to the School Library*, p. 112.

[184] Source: Jim Harmon, *The Great Radio Comedians*, pp. 95-96.

[185] Source: Kathleen Krull, *Lives of the Athletes*, pp. 71, 73.

[186] Source: John D. Evans, *A Tom Sawyer Companion*, p. 59.

[187] Source: Simon Doonan, *Wacky Chicks*, pp. 229-230.

[188] Source: Michael Cain, *Louise Nevelson*, p. 95.

[189] Source: Helen White Charles, collector and editor, *Quaker Chuckles*, Preface.

[190] Source: Jack Kinney, *Walt Disney and Other Assorted Characters*, p. 188.

[191] Source: Liza Donnelly, *Funny Ladies*, p. 17.

[192] Source: Eddie Shapiro, "Desperate Dishing." 2 October 2005 <http://www2.out.com/detail.asp?id=13384>.

[193] Source: Dick Van Dyke, *Those Funny Kids!*, p. 128.

[194] Source: David Blum, *Quintet: Five Journeys Toward Musical Fulfillment*, p. 89.

[195] Source: Joan Hammond, *A Voice, A Life*, p. 163.

[196] Source: Cal and Rose Samra, editors, *More Holy Humor*, p. 35.

[197] Source: David Ewen, *Dictators of the Baton*, pp. 185-186.

[198] Source: Molly/Monica Gedeon.

[199] Source: Chan Hon Goh, *Beyond the Dance: A Ballerina's Life*, pp. 25-27.

[200] Source: The Right Reverend V. Gene Robinson, "Giving Away Our Fears." 25 October 2005 <http://www.advocate.com/exclusive_detail_ektid21941.asp>.

[201] Source: Tomie dePaola, *Here We All Are*, pp. 18-19.

[202] Source: Donald J. Sobol, *Encyclopedia Brown's Book of Wacky Sports*, pp. 111-112.

[203] Source: Joseph Epstein, " The Many Faces of Celebrity Philanthropy." *In Character*. "Generosity" issue. Spring 2006 <http://www.incharacter.org/article.php?article=65>.

[204] Source: "Jillette Names Daughter Moxie CrimeFighter." 4 June 2005 <http://entertainment.tv.yahoo.com/entnews/ap/20050604/111792564000.html>.

[205] Source: Carolyn Daffron, *Edna St. Vincent Millay*, p. 21.

[206] Source: Jim Harmon, *The Great Radio Comedians*, p. 179.

[207] Source: Michèle Brown and Ann O'Connor, *Hammer and Tongues*, pp. 111-112.

[208] Source: Kate Clinton, *What the L?*, p. 77, 79-80.

[209] Source: Bob Dole, *Great Presidential Wit*, p. 66.

[210] Source: William Bramhall, *The Great American Misfit*, pp. 47-48.

[211] Source: Sanford Pinsker, "The physics classroom where science and superstition met." 28 October 2005 <http://irascibleprofessor.com/comments-10-28-05.htm>.

[212] Source: Mark Sufrin, *Payton*, pp. 44-45.

[213] Source: Tom Mullen, *Living Longer and Other Sobering Possibilities*, p. 60.

[214] Source: Beth Lisick, *Everybody into the Pool*, pp. 41, 49.

[215] Source: John Anthony Scott, *Fanny Kemble's America*, pp. 78-80.

[216] Source: Don L. Wulffson, *Amazing True Stories*, pp. 11-12.

[217] Source: Barbara Diamond Goldin, *A Child's Book of the Midrash: 52 Jewish Stories from the Sages*, pp. 72-74.

[218] Source: Lawrence J. Epstein, *A Treasury of Jewish Inspirational Stories*, pp. 55-56.

[219] Source: Michael A. Sommers, *Chris Crutcher*, p. 17.

[220] Source: Gregg Lewis and Deborah Shaw Lewis, *Today's Heroes: Joni Eareckson Tada*, p. 81.

[221] Source: Mary Kathleen Glavich, S.N.D., *Catholic School Kids Say the Funniest Things*, p. 80.

[222] Source: Donald J. Sobol, *Encyclopedia Brown's Book of Wacky Sports*, p. 97.

[223] Source: Judy L. Hasday, *Agnes de Mille*, p. 34.

[224] Source: Margaret Speaker-Yuan, *Agnes de Mille*, p. 67.

[225] Source: David Ewen, *Dictators of the Baton*, p. 182.

[226] Source: Bob Dole, *Great Presidential Wit*, p. 97.

[227] Source: Emily Yoffe, "My Mommy War." 14 June 2006 <www.slate.com/id/2143659/?nav=tap3>.

[228] Source: Carl Erskine, *Carl Erskine's Tales from the Dodger Dugout*, p. 31.

[229] Source: Carolyn Daffron, *Edna St. Vincent Millay*, p. 25.

[230] Source: Frank B. Gilbreth, Jr. and Ernestine Gilbreth Carey, *Belles on Their Toes*, p. 171.

[231] Source: Joe Garner, *Stay Tuned: Television's Unforgettable Moments*, p. 25.

[232] Source: Robert Lipsyte, *Assignment: Sports*, pp. 171-172.

[233] Source: Nancy Shore, *Amelia Earhart*, p. 72.

[234] Source: "Man Who Delivers 113-Page Marriage Proposal Gets One-Word Answer." 14 February 2006 <http://www.lulu.com/static/pr/01_14_06.php>.

[235] Source: Lorna Williams, "The joys of Julia and her mastering of French cuisine." 29 May 2006 <http://www.washingtontimes.com/books/20060506-112345-1245r.htm>.

[236] Source: Meg Cabot, *Perfect Princess*, pp. 5-9.

[237] Source: Meg Cabot, "Gramps." 6 December 2005 <http://www.megcabot.com/diary/post.cfm/pid/2330 >.

[238] Source: Netzach, editor, *Chesed: The World is Built upon Kindness*, p. 20.

[239] Source: Rabbi Joseph H. Gelberman, *Zen Judaism: Teaching Tales of a Kabbalistic Rabbi*, p. 107. The pages of this volume are unnumbered, but I started counting with the Introduction as page 1.

[240] Source: Barbara O'Connor, *Barefoot Dancer: The Story of Isadora Duncan*, pp. 74, 78-79.

[241] Source: Morris N. Kertzer, *Tell Me, Rabbi*, p. 39.

[242] Source: Lawrence J. Epstein, *A Treasury of Jewish Inspirational Stories*, p. 128.

[243] Source: Morris N. Kertzer, *Tell Me, Rabbi*, p. 33.

[244] Source: Bart Rockwell, *World's Strangest Football Stories*, p. 86.

[245] Source: David Blum, *Quintet: Five Journeys Toward Musical Fulfillment*, p. 94.

[246] Source: Alan Govenar, collector and editor, *Stompin' at the Savoy: The Story of Norma Miller*, pp. 2-3.

[247] Source: Mary E. Lyons, editor, *Talking with Tebé: Clementine Hunter, Memory Artist*, p. 6.

[248] Source: Linda Gambee Henry and James Douglas Henry, *The Soul of the Caring Nurse*, p. 55.

[249] Source: Michael A. Schuman, *Halle Berry: "Beauty is Not Just Physical,"* pp. 10-11, 17-18.

[250] Source: Lawrence J. Epstein, *Mixed Nuts*, p. 41.